the
kingdom. Our church
thanks you for the
privilege of
participating in
your work.

Grace & Peace,

Eric Porterfield

SESSIONS WITH GALATIANS

Smyth & Helwys Publishing, Inc.
6316 Peake Road
Macon, Georgia 31210-3960
1-800-747-3016
© 2005 by Smyth & Helwys Publishing
All rights reserved.
Printed in the United States of America.

The paper used in this publication meets the minimum
requirements of American National Standard for Information
Sciences—Permanence of Paper for Printed Library Materials.

Library of Congress Cataloging-in-Publication Data

Porterfield, Eric, 1967-
Sessions with Galatians : finding freedom through Christ / Eric Porterfield.
p. cm.
ISBN 1-57312-446-X (pbk. : alk. paper)
1. Bible. N.T. Galatians—Criticism, interpretation, etc.
I. Title.
BS2685.52.P67 2005
227'.406--dc22

2005006518

Sessions *with* Galatians

Finding Freedom *through* Christ

Eric S. Porterfield

SMYTH&HELWYS
PUBLISHING, INCORPORATED · MACON, GEORGIA

Table of Contents

Acknowlegments v

Introducing Galatians vii

Session 1 1
Freedom from the Present Evil Age

Session 2 11
Paul's Personal Testimony

Session 3 21
The Church of Two Tables

Session 4 29
The Faith of Jesus Christ

Session 5 37
The Supremacy of Faith

Session 6 47
Promise Fulfilled

Session 7 55
Freed Slaves, Adopted Children, and Friends

Session 8 65
The Only Thing That Matters

Session 9 75
The Spirit Versus the Flesh

Session 10 87
Fruit on Display

Bibliography 97

Acknowledgments

. . . The influence of Richard Hays is evident on every page of these sessions. His commentary in *The New Interpreter's Bible* was the primary reference point for my own interpretation. J. Louis Martyn's commentary from *The Anchor Bible* series shaped my understanding of "the present evil age" and "the flesh." Mark Baker's *Religious No More* pointed me to a relational understanding of justification. My interpretation of Galatians 3:10-14 is built on N. T. Wright's work in *The Climax of the Covenant.* Session 9 on the fruit of the Spirit was greatly influenced by Philip Kenneson's *Life on the Vine.*

. . . These sessions were enhanced and strengthened by Vern Peterson, Alicia Davis Porterfied, and Peggy Womble, who read the text and made valuable suggestions.

. . . The congregation of the First Baptist Church of Sanford, North Carolina, first heard these sessions in sermonic form. I am humbled by and thankful for their encouragement, interest, and support.

. . . For the privilege of sharing these words in print, I am grateful to Keith Gammons and his associates at Smyth & Helwys, and to Michael McCullar, series editor.

. . . For the privilege of trying to live these words with Alicia, Davis, and Luke, I give thanks to God.

Introducing Galatians

As the Pittsburgh Pirates baseball team marched toward a World Series championship in 1979, a disco dance tune emerged as their theme song: "We Are Family." The Pirates' story involved more than a sports team bonding on the field and in the clubhouse. A whole city united around its heroes. Steel workers and mill owners, labor and management sang the same song. Blue collar and white collar, black and white cheered the same team. For one season at least, the barriers that kept people apart came down and all could sing, "We are family!"

"We are family" should be the universal song of the church. Jesus tears down the barriers that human beings construct between themselves and creates a new family of sisters and brothers in Christ. But too often we prefer the old ways of separation and insist that other believers "become as we are" before being considered "one of us." Paul wrote the Letter to the Galatians at a time when many Jewish Christians believed that Gentiles (the Jewish term for non-Jews) must embrace the practices and rituals of Judaism before they could truly become part of God's people. Often called the "works of the law," these practices included circumcision, strict Sabbath observance, dietary laws, and the recognition of special holy days. Believing in Jesus was not enough if a Gentile wanted to be part of the family.

After Paul founded churches in Galatia and then continued his missionary journeys, rival Jewish Christian missionaries told the Galatians that obedience to the Jewish law must be added to their faith in Christ. To Paul's horror, the Galatians were listening. Paul argued with every fiber of his being that Jesus incorporates all who follow him into one family, regardless of whether or not they performed the works of the law. His letter was an urgent effort to refocus the Galatians' attention solely on the faith of Jesus Christ.

The Churches of Galatia

The battlefield where Paul and his opponents squared off was a Roman province called Galatia, a region in modern Turkey. The name "Galatia" comes not from the land itself but from the people who settled the land in the third century BC. This group originated in the Danube River region of central Europe and migrated into western Europe, the Balkans, and finally Asia Minor (Turkey). They were known as Celts in Britain, Gauls in France, and Galatians in Asia Minor. The word "Galatia" means "the land of the Greek-speaking Gauls" (Longenecker, lxii).

The Galatians settled in the highlands of Anatolia, around modern Ankara. In 25 BC, the Romans gained control of the region and created the province of Galatia, applying the name to an area larger than the lands occupied by ethnic Galatians. Territory to the south became part of the Galatian province, including the cities of Lystra and Derbe that Paul visited in Acts 14:1-23 (Hays, 191).

Paul founded churches in the southern portion of the Galatian province during his first missionary journey (Acts 13–14). He founded churches among the ethnic Galatians of the north during his second missionary journey (Acts 16:6), and he visited them again in Acts 18:23. When Paul writes "to the churches of Galatia" (1:2), we do not know if he refers to the ethnic Galatians of the north or to the non-ethnic Galatians in the south. However, for the purpose of understanding their story, their identity as Gentiles matters more than their location. Paul addressed Gentiles who received the gospel through his ministry, then fell under the influence of rival missionaries who preached a gospel of Christ plus the law.

The Date of Galatians

According to Luke's chronology in Acts, Paul participated in the "Jesusalem conference" (Acts 15) between his visits to southern and northern Galatia. This conference was held to debate Gentile inclusion in the church, and Paul describes his role in Galatians 2:1-10. Scholars believe the conference took place in AD 48 or 49. If the Galatian churches were founded during the years before and after the Jerusalem conference, and allowing time for the rival missionaries to challenge Paul's law-free message and for Paul to hear the challenge, we can guess that Paul wrote his letter in the mid-50s (Hays, 193).

The Occasion

Roughly twenty years after the resurrection of Jesus, the gospel had spread into Asia Minor. Many Gentiles now followed Israel's Messiah. In response, many Jewish Christians asked, "Must Gentiles keep the law, or is faith in Jesus sufficient for their entrance into God's family?"

Rival missionaries to the Galatian province vehemently disagreed over the question's answer. As the founding missionary, Paul urged the Galatians to maintain their embrace of the faith-based gospel he preached. His opponents, whom we will call the Missionaries, sought to convert the Galatians to a law-based message.

In the Letter to the Galatians, Paul wrestles rivals who distort the gospel and defame his character. He fights to save the churches he has worked so hard to establish. Far from an abstract, systematic theological statement delivered in a scholarly debate, Galatians is a specific response to a specific crisis. Paul pleads with friends who are unknowingly walking away from Jesus, believing that God will lead them back to the truth of the gospel.

Freedom from the Present Evil Age

Galatians 1:1-5

The preacher stands before the church and opens the Bible. The congregation, gathered in Jesus' name, believes God will speak a word to them as the word is read and proclaimed. In our hearts we ask, "What word does God have for us today?"

A church leader stands before a congregation in Galatia and opens Paul's letter. The anticipation dwarfs anything we experience before present-day sermons, even at our attentive best. As they gather on the Lord's Day to sing and pray, we can imagine the first recipients of his letter asking, "What word does God have for us through our brother Paul?"

Just as we expect God to move among us when the word is proclaimed, so Paul expected God to act in Galatia when his letter was read. Paul believed God would change the hearts and minds of those who listened.

The Defense Begins

"Paul an apostle—sent neither by human commission nor from human authorities, but through Jesus Christ and God the Father, who raised him from the dead . . ." (1:1). As the first sentence is read, attentive Galatian listeners most likely feel exposed and discovered. With these beginning words, Paul lets them know that *he* knows; he knows they are listening to rival Missionaries who question his authority. Perhaps the Missionaries asked, "Was Paul truly an apostle set apart by Jesus, or was he set apart by himself or some other human authority? Can he be trusted?" Instead of rejecting the questions, the Galatians made the questions their own.

As we shall see in 1:11-24, the Missionaries imply that Paul learned the gospel from the apostles in Jerusalem and then changed the message without their approval. Paul insists that no human commission or authority sent him to preach. He has no obligation to follow any "party line" or please any constituency. Sent by the Father through Jesus, Paul's only aim is to please God. When it comes to the source of his call and the content of his message, he looks to God and God alone.

Christ's Gift

Though set apart by God through Jesus Christ and not by any human authority, Paul remains connected to his sisters and brothers in Christ. He writes not as an isolated individual but as a person in community, bringing greetings from "all the brothers and sisters who are with me" (1:2). The larger Christian community shapes his thinking. When Paul speaks of Jesus, "who gave himself for our sins" (1:4), many scholars believe he borrows from an early Christian hymn. Since Paul wrote for congregations in which the praises of God were sung, borrowing from a familiar hymn would have been an appropriate literary move. Regardless of its source, v. 4 performs a hymn-like function by concisely articulating the community's core beliefs. We sing our faith to help us understand our faith, and Paul used a hymn-like refrain to define the gospel he preached.

Human beings were created to live in right relationship with God, with each other, and with all creation. Human sin disrupts these relationships, and because of our sinfulness, we cannot make our relationships "right." Jesus "gave himself for our sins" when he died on the cross, taking upon himself the sin that separates us from God and each other. At the cross, Jesus took the initiative, reaching out to a creation that rejected its creator. On the cross, God's determination to live in relationship with humanity was on display. Jesus "gave himself for our sins" to create a new family in which love for God, neighbor, and creation reigns.

The Present Evil Age

On the cross, Jesus did more than forgive individual sins. He defeated the power of sin in order "to set us free from the present evil age" (1:4). Paul divides human history into two ages—the present evil age in which sin has dominion, and the age to come in which God will reign completely and sin will be no more. Paul personifies the present evil age, saying it has the power to enslave human beings and shape them according to its will. More than a description of the way things are, "the present evil age" is a force from which human beings must be liberated. The present evil age leads people away from love of God, neighbor, and creation. Human beings remain responsible for their sins, but they live in an age that shapes them to be sinners.

The New Testament identifies numerous agents that do the work of the present evil age. In Galatians, Paul focuses on the "elemental spirits of the world" (4:3, 9; see Session 7) and "the flesh" (5:16; see Session 9). Paul does not envision demons invading and possessing individuals, with each person a puppet in the devil's hands. Instead, Paul sees the elemental spirits and the flesh at work within larger corporate structures of human existence. He identifies areas in which the elemental spirits have corrupted both pagan and Israelite religious systems and shows how the flesh sows dissension and discord within congregations. But the influence of these agents is not limited to religions and churches. Governmental, economic, and cultural systems fall prey to the corrupting influence of the elemental spirits and the flesh, so that nations, communities, and individuals are shaped to be compliant citizens of the present evil age.

Confronted by the horrors of Nazi Germany, Dietrich Bonhoeffer wrote, "How can one close one's eyes at the fact that the demons themselves have taken over rule of the world, that it is the powers of darkness who have here made an awful conspiracy?" (Dawn, 8). In 1930s Germany, good Christian people endorsed, empowered, and followed an evil leader. Our German sisters and brothers remain responsible for their active or implicit endorsement of Nazi rule. They also were shaped by the present evil age to walk down a destructive and genocidal path, all in the name of national glory.

In the same vein, how could slavery and segregation be endorsed, sanctioned, and defended in what is known in America as the Bible Belt? All who benefited from, participated in, or did not speak out against this system are responsible for their own sinful actions. They were also influenced by the present evil age that works against the purposes of God. They were people of great faithfulness and great sinfulness, just as we are. They were unable to overcome the influence of the present evil age in their corporate lives, and thus they individually participated in an evil system.

On the cross, Jesus invaded the present evil age and set us free from its power! He does not transport us out of this age or make us immune to its influence, but frees us from its ability to dominate our lives. People who gave witness to a power greater than Hitler, slavery, and segregation lived out of a spiritual freedom that the Gestapo, slavery, and Jim Crow could not take away. Such lives of freedom are made possible by the cross, follow the pattern of the cross, and point others to the cross.

The New Creation

In his introductory remarks, Paul celebrates Christ's gift of freedom from the present evil age. In his concluding remarks, he celebrates the new creation (6:15) brought into being through Christ. The two images serve as bookends for the entire letter. In the new creation, life exists according to God's will so that people live in right relationship with God, each other, and all creation. Though the new creation will not be fully revealed until Christ returns, it is already present in the world. The new creation is visible from within the present evil age whenever God's will is done "on earth as it is in heaven."

The task of the church is to give witness to God's new creation in the midst of the present evil age. Slowly but surely, the Spirit-empowered church advances further into the turf of the present evil age, but not through the means of this age. With the cross as the example, the church takes territory not by violence but through sacrificial service. The church relies on overwhelming love, not overpowering force. Instead of dominating the world from above, the church subverts the present evil age from within as salt and light and yeast in the dough.

By insisting that Gentiles follow the law, the Missionaries of Paul's day remained firmly planted in the present evil age. Keeping the rules mattered more to them than Christ's liberating work. If the Galatians followed the Missionaries, they would enter slavery to the law, another form of slavery to the present evil age. If they remained focused on Jesus, however, they would experience a taste of God's new creation. They would give witness to the new creation through lives of faithfulness and love.

Doxology

After celebrating grace and freedom with a hymn-like refrain in v. 4, Paul ends his introduction with a doxology of praise to God the Father, "to whom be the glory forever and ever. Amen." In response to the liberating grace of Jesus received according to the will of the

Father and experienced through the presence of the Spirit, Paul gives glory to God. No mention is made of a debt human beings must repay because of what Christ has done, nor is there any suggestion that human beings must make themselves worthy of Christ's work. God has bestowed an undeserved gift on humanity, and the human response is to give praise to the Giver.

With the word, "amen," Paul establishes his letter as an act of worship. Author and recipients are co-participants in an offering to God. The word "amen" is not a means for ending a particular train of thought, nor does it signify the conclusion of a personal prayer. The "amen" draws the Galatians and Paul together into God's presence. The "amen" flows from Paul's "conviction that his own words can and will become the active word of God, because God will be present as the letter is read to the Galatians in their services of worship" (Martyn, 106).

Theologian Marva Dawn begins her lectures and sermons by extending her arms to the audience/congregation and saying, "The Lord be with you." With arms extended, the audience/congregation responds, "And also with you." She writes, "We say these phrases to remember that we are a community listening to God together. I can't teach well if those present don't work on the topic with me side by side." The listener response is a commitment of participation in the words that follow (Dawn and Peterson, 10).

We do not know if the Galatians joined Paul in saying "amen" at the conclusion of 1:5. But such a response would have been appropriate and consistent with Paul's intentions. If they were not already anticipating a word from God, Paul's "amen" jolted the Galatians awake and raised the stakes. What follows are not simply greetings from a beloved brother or teachings from their founding pastor. The reading of Paul's letter was an event in which God would speak. God would do something through Paul's words, and the Galatians had to decide if they would be open to the Spirit's movement in their midst.

Life Lessons

North American Christians tend to view the gospel in individualistic terms, so in 1:4 we expect Paul to speak of Jesus, "who gave himself for our sins so that we might experience forgiveness of our sins." Paul calls our individualistic focus into question when he instead says Jesus "gave himself for our sins *to set us free from the present evil age.*" The forgiveness of our personal sins is certainly included in Christ's rescue, but Paul's emphasis is corporate. On the cross, Jesus defeated the present evil age and all its agents and *created a people* who give witness to the new creation. One of the church's Spirit-empowered gifts is the ability to recognize the present evil age.

Two extremes characterize the way modern Christians approach Paul's talk of "the present evil age," "the elemental spirits of the world," and "the flesh." Some Christians see the devil at work in every area of our lives, invading our thoughts, twisting our actions, and manipulating our circumstances. Others locate evil spiritual forces within an outdated ancient world-view. Whenever the Bible speaks of such forces, the terms must be translated "into categories more readily available and comprehensible to the modern mind." Both approaches enable us to "*evade* rather than engage the disturbing things" Paul says about the present evil age (Harink, 74). The first approach over-personalizes the demonic and the second dismisses it, but either way, the power of corporate evil is not addressed.

Rather than personalizing the demonic or translating it into modern terms, why not take Paul's terms at face value? The suffering, violence, and hatred of the world are too great to attribute solely to human sinfulness. We need only look at the newspapers for evidence of a "present evil age" that works against the purposes of God.

The church recognizes the present evil age when its life is shaped by corporate worship. As we pray, sing, and hear God's word read and proclaimed, God speaks and awakens us to the present evil age and its influence. The new creation is revealed as the church offers itself to God in worship, and the congregation is shaped to give witness to that creation as we depart and go into the world.

1. Paul appeals to God's call in his life as the authority for his message. We rightly are skeptical when people assert authority over us after hearing a "word from God." How can churches balance respect for God's personal call on individuals (clergy or laity) while recognizing that God speaks to people not as isolated individuals but as people-in-community?

_____

_____

_____

_____

_____

_____

_____

_____

_____

2. What difference does it make, if any, that Paul writes on behalf of "all the members of God's family who are with me"? (1:2)

_____

_____

_____

_____

_____

_____

_____

_____

3. Would you have expected Paul to say Jesus "gave himself for our sins that our sins might be forgiven"? If so, why?

_____

_____

_____

_____

_____

_____

_____

4. What is your understanding of the demonic in the New Testament and in our world today?

_____
_____
_____
_____
_____
_____
_____

5. What are some historical examples in which it seems the present evil age was at work in a particular government or culture?

_____
_____
_____
_____
_____
_____
_____

6. All governments, economies, and cultures are vulnerable to the present evil age. In what areas do you think the United States government, economy, and culture reflect the present evil age? Where can we see the new creation in these same structures?

_____
_____
_____
_____
_____
_____
_____

7. In what specific ways does your church give witness to the new creation? Are there areas in your church's life that reflect the present evil age more than the new creation?

_____

_____

_____

_____

_____

_____

_____

8. Describe a worship service in which you participated where the congregation experienced a glimpse of the new creation.

_____

_____

_____

_____

_____

_____

_____

Paul's Personal Testimony

Galatians 1:6-24

After the introductory paragraph of his letters, Paul normally gives thanks for his audience. Following his greetings to the Philippians, he writes, "I thank my God every time I remember you, constantly praying with joy in every one of my prayers for all of you" (Phil 1:3-4). Instead of a section of thanksgiving and joy, the Galatians receive anger and curses. The anger implicit in Paul's introductory greetings becomes undeniably explicit as he writes, "I am astonished that you are so quickly deserting the one who called you in the grace of Christ and are turning to a different gospel" (1:6). By this point in the worship service, surely Paul's letter had attracted the undivided attention of the congregation.

The "one who called you" refers to God, not Paul. Though Paul feels personally betrayed (4:15-16), of greater concern was the Galatians' wavering faith. The Missionaries diluted God's call when they required law observance and gave the Galatians a list of things to do. By their very nature, checklists focus on human effort and achievement, fitting nicely into the present evil age and its effort to distract people from God. God called the Galatians—and God calls us—away from a focus on human achievement, emphasizing instead Christ's achievement on the cross. Deserting this call denies that Jesus set us free from the present evil age, removes the cross from the center of God's work in the world, and ultimately denies the existence of the new creation.

The Missionaries in Paul's day did not introduce a different, but acceptable, way of understanding the gospel. They perverted and domesticated the gospel so that it did not disrupt the present evil age. Paul resisted this perversion with the strongest language possible, calling down God's curse on the Missionaries and all who would distort the gospel message (1:8-9).

Escape from Religion

We have no record of the charges Paul's opponents made against him, but we can make good guesses of what they were based on how Paul responds in Galatians. Paul denies that he is seeking human approval or trying to please people, suggesting that his opponents accused him of doing these very things (1:10). Most likely, the opponents said Paul told people what they wanted to hear, leaving out difficult requirements like circumcision. The Missionaries claimed that Paul watered down the message, sacrificing its content in exchange for the Galatians' approval and affection.

At an earlier time in his life, these charges would have been accurate, but they missed the mark now that Paul followed Jesus. He states, "If I were still pleasing people, I would not be a servant of Christ." In 1:14 Paul recalls that earlier time when human approval directed his life and received his energy. "I advanced in Judaism beyond many among my people of the same age, for I was far more zealous for the traditions of my ancestors," he admits. Paul aimed to impress others by his religious activity. Judaism provided an arena of competition where he could make a name for himself by being better than his peers. But when God called him and revealed Jesus to him (1:15), Paul put aside his quest for human approval and dedicated himself to pleasing God. He rejected his human-centered "religion" when God revealed to him the living faith of Jesus.

The word "Judaism" developed under the Greek cultural influence of Paul's day to distinguish the religion of the Jews from other ancient religions in the Hellenistic world. The only time the word is used in the New Testament is in 1:13-14. The term is cultural instead of doctrinal in nature, describing Jewish practices instead of beliefs. In Paul's usage, "Judaism" does not describe the living faith of Israel but a religious system from which Jesus set him free.

Judaism as a religious system distracted people from the God of Abraham, Isaac, and Jacob and turned their attention instead to practices like circumcision, Sabbath observance, and dietary restrictions. Instead of reliance upon God, Judaism encouraged self-reliance. Instead of cooperation, it produced competition. One could excel at keeping the practices of Judaism, advancing beyond one's peers and thus gaining the approval of the religious community. Instead of a community that welcomed the stranger and the outsider, Judaism encouraged a circling of the wagons to keep the stranger out. The practices of Judaism set Jews apart from Gentiles, establishing who was "out" and who was "in."

In Galatians, we read that the Missionaries believe Jesus is the Messiah of Israel, but they do not believe Christ's messianic reign makes the practices of Judaism optional. In their teaching, Paul sees a return to "religion" and a rejection of the living faith of Christ. By imposing the practices of Judaism on the followers of Christ, the Missionaries create another environment where people can excel in competition with others and where boundaries can be rigidly drawn to maintain an exclusive community.

Instead of experiencing the freedom of the new creation, the Missionaries are still enslaved to the present evil age. Instead of preparing people's hearts to receive God's gifts, the Missionaries view the practices of Judaism as a means to gaining approval, both human and divine. They domesticate the gospel of Christ, accommodating his life, death, and resurrection into their old way of thinking instead of allowing Christ to transform their thinking. Paul once had the same aversion to the idea that God would do something so radically new that it could not be held within the bounds of his "religion." He violently persecuted the church and tried to destroy it because it threatened his human-centered vision of faith. Now he recognizes the threat of domestication the Missionaries pose to the gospel, and he resists them with all his might.

A Word Against Anti-Semitism

The continuing influence of the present evil age and the evidence of enduring human sinfulness are made frighteningly clear in the church's persecution of the Jews. Because of his attacks on "Judaism" in Galatians, Paul's letter has often been abused to endorse and condone this persecution. We must vigilantly remember the distinction Paul made between "Judaism" and the faith of Israel. Paul opposed a dogmatic system of religious practices, not the living faith of the Jewish people that nurtured him and prepared him for his ministry. He did not condemn Jewish practices, but condemned the practice of making them mandatory for church membership. Paul wrote Galatians as a Jew, and he based his arguments for the gospel on the Jewish Scriptures (Gal 3:6-29; 4:21–5:1). Paul called "accursed" anyone who perverted the gospel. He did not call the people of Israel "accursed." When anti-Semitism rears its ugly head among followers of Jesus, life in Christ's new creation has been exchanged for slavery to the present evil age.

Defending His Call

Paul received the gospel he preached through a direct revelation from God; it was not of human origin (1:11-12). His opponents doubted the story of his call, charging instead that Paul learned the gospel from the Jerusalem apostles and then watered it down. In 1:16-24 Paul says this charge has no basis in fact, since he did not visit Jerusalem until three years after his call, and even then his visit was short (1:18). If Paul was unknown at the time by sight to the churches of Judea (1:22), then how is it possible that he learned the gospel from the leaders of those churches?

Though the geographical facts conclusively make Paul's case, the most important evidence is theological. God's call is not simply a new assignment or even the source of Paul's new direction in life. Just as God invaded the present evil age through the life, death, and resurrection of Jesus, God invaded Paul's life when "God was pleased to reveal his Son to me" (1:16). This invasion took place according to the will of God the Father, since God had set Paul apart before he was born (1:15).

If Paul the Pharisee had followed Jesus by his own choice, surely he would have followed the same path as the Missionaries and simply added faith in Jesus to his existing practices. How could Paul make up a gospel that has no place for the practices of Judaism? Only a direct invasion by God could erase a lifetime of training in righteous achievement and create a new life of receiving righteousness through Jesus. Nothing short of a revelation from God could have pulled Paul out of his Jewish exclusiveness and sent him into the Gentile world, proclaiming a law-free gospel based not on human effort but on the gift of Christ's faithfulness.

Jerusalem-approved

If anyone in Galatia still questioned Paul's apostleship after hearing the geographical and theological evidence, Paul removed all reason for doubt when he revealed his Jerusalem endorsement. The Missionaries said Paul learned the gospel from the apostles and then watered it down, when in fact the Jerusalem apostles had acknowledged his apostleship and put their stamp of approval on his message.

The circumstances by which Paul received this endorsement are quite similar to the current situation in Galatia. In 2:1-10 Paul remembers a controversy in Antioch that was resolved by a council in Jerusalem. Acts 15:1 describes the controversy, stating, "Then certain individuals came from Judea and were teaching the brothers, 'Unless you are circumcised according to the custom of Moses, you cannot be saved.'" In the excitement of the church's growth beyond the borders of Israel, the church at Antioch had somehow found a way to keep Jewish and Gentile Christians together in one body. This progressive spirit did not sit well with many in the mother church, thus the visit from the Judean individuals with their demands for Gentile circumcision.

It comes as no surprise that Paul had "no small dissension and debate with them" (Acts 15:2), and the church at Antioch sent Paul and Barnabas to Jerusalem to settle the question of Gentile circumcision. Galatians 2:1-10 describes the subsequent council involving the apostle to the Gentiles and the Jerusalem apostles. Paul and Barnabas intentionally include Titus as a traveling companion (2:1). Titus is a Gentile Christian, and whether or not he is accepted in Jerusalem as a brother in Christ will reveal the atmosphere in the mother church. The apostles do not compel Titus to be circumcised (2:3), providing the first indication that Paul's message will be endorsed.

"Those leaders contributed nothing to me" (2:6) is Paul's version of the minutes of his actual private meeting with the Jerusalem apostles. Paul has in mind the current charge that the apostles taught him the gospel. He refutes the Missionaries, saying the Jerusalem apostles added nothing to the message he now proclaims. The apostles agreed that what Paul proclaims is the true gospel. Gentiles do not have to be circumcised according to the custom of Moses in order to be saved.

As the earlier meeting concluded, James, Cephas (Peter), and John extended to Paul and Barnabas the right hand of fellowship (2:9), signaling not only their acceptance of Paul's law-free gospel, but also acknowledging Paul as an apostle. They did not bestow apostleship on Paul but recognized the apostleship he had already received from God. The Missionaries have their story wrong; they claim to represent the message of the Jerusalem church when in reality, the apostle Paul is the one with Jerusalem's endorsement.

Not everyone in Jerusalem rejoiced in the apostolic handshakes. A small faction in the Jerusalem church unsuccessfully attempted to disrupt the council and discredit Paul (2:4-5). The council did not settle once and for all the questions of how Gentiles were to be included in the church, for the "circumcision faction" would soon cause trouble in Antioch again (2:11-14). The Missionaries' presence in Galatia shows that this faction is very much alive several years after the council. The fact that Paul must write Galatians after the Jerusalem council's endorsement of his message reminds us that consensus regarding the Gentile mission was a long time in coming.

Unity Amid Diversity

Paul's description of the Jerusalem council reflects his desire for a clear and unified vision in the church's Gentile mission. As signified by his curse of the Missionaries, he considers out of bounds those who require circumcision of Gentile Christians. Such people are "false believers" (2:4) and like the Missionaries must be resisted in order to preserve Gentile freedom in Christ.

In Jerusalem, Paul laid the gospel he proclaimed before the Jerusalem apostles "in order to make sure that I was not running, or had not run, in vain" (2:2). He did not doubt the correctness of his position. Lack of endorsement from the apostles would not affect his confidence in his calling from God. His course would be in vain if the apostles did not share his vision, necessitating a parting of the ways and the existence of two separate churches—one for Jews and the other for Gentiles.

Paul did not seek personal affirmation and a pat on the back during his visit to Jerusalem. He sought unity on the core message of the gospel so that the church could continue the new creation's advance into territory still claimed by the present evil age. Endorsement by the apostles certainly makes Paul's work easier, and he does not hesitate in using their endorsement to further his case with the Galatians. But of greater importance is the apostles' recognition of what God is actually doing among the Gentiles. New creation is happening beyond the boundaries of Israel. The Jerusalem apostles realized that God was at work in ways they had not envisioned. Even as they continued their own work among the circumcised, their vision of the gospel expanded through their recognition that Paul had been entrusted with the gospel for the uncircumcised (2:7).

Even as Paul and the Jerusalem apostles pursue their separate callings, they cannot live lives of complete separation. One group ministers to Jews and the other to Gentiles, but they remain members of the same family. The council experience affirmed and solidified their family connection, and the Jerusalem apostles pointed to this connection when they asked Paul to remember the poor.

The apostolic request referred specifically to the poor in Jerusalem. For various reasons, the Jerusalem Christians often found themselves in financial difficulty. The mother church from which the earliest missionaries were sent came to depend on the churches she birthed. Paul expresses his eagerness to comply with Jerusalem's request for help in Galatians 2:10. He stands by this commitment, for he is raising money for Jerusalem when he says the words we so often use in stewardship campaigns: "Each of you must give as you have made up your mind, not reluctantly or under compulsion, for God loves a cheerful giver" (2 Cor 9:7).

Life Lessons

The Missionaries charged Paul with seeking the approval of others. I suspect many of us are guilty of the same charge. More than we care to admit, our lifestyles, actions, and words are influenced by how we think others will perceive us. God delivers us from such thinking as we allow God's call to determine our lives. The call to follow Jesus communicates God's love for the world (including us) and creates a new creation in which we are invited to participate. In the new creation, the need to compete with others and advance beyond our peers disappears. The more we allow God's call to reveal our presence in the new creation, the less concerned we become for the approval of others.

In service to our need for approval, we create checklists by which we compare ourselves to others. How well a person keeps the checklists of a particular culture determines how others perceive that person. In my own tradition, the weekly offering envelopes often have a checklist, indicating whether or not a person has read his or her Bible and Sunday school lesson during the week. Personal Bible study and preparation for Sunday school are important spiritual disciplines, but if they become something to check off a "to-do" list or a way to be more spiritual than the person who left that item blank, they are human-centered religious acts, not responses to the living God.

For many churches, the mental checklists may include how a person dresses, whether or not a person is considered "nice" and "easy to get along with," and whether or not a person hangs out with the "right kind of people." Political loyalties or positions on social issues often find their way into checklists. Theological uniformity is a perennial checklist standard. While such issues may need consideration depending on the context, they must not be used to exclude individuals from the people of God.

Because we are sinners, checklists will be a part of church life until the new creation is fully revealed. Thankfully, God works among us and through us in spite of our checklists. Paul and the Jerusalem apostles acknowledged that God called them to different areas of ministry (2:7-9). Both groups were imperfect sinners trying to follow Jesus as best they could. As we argue with churches and Christians that have different checklists than ours, it is good to remember that if God can work through imperfect sinners like us, then God can work through the people with whom we strongly disagree.

1. In what ways do you find yourself pleasing people instead of seeking God's approval?

_____
_____
_____
_____
_____

2. What are the checklists you carry around in your heart as a means to earn the approval of others?

_____
_____
_____
_____
_____

3. What are the checklists at your church or other churches you know that one must follow in order to be considered part of the "in" crowd?

_____
_____
_____
_____
_____

4. In what ways do checklists create competition between individuals, between churches, and between denominations?

_____
_____
_____
_____
_____

5. How could Paul's commitment to the practices of Judaism and zeal for his religious heritage lead him to violently persecute the church?

_____
_____
_____
_____
_____

6. Paul leaves no room for compromise with the Missionaries, cursing them (1:8-9) and calling their peers "false believers" (2:4). What are the beliefs and practices so crucial to following Jesus that without them, a person or church has ceased to be Christian?

_____
_____
_____
_____
_____

7. What are the areas where different churches or individuals within the same church can "agree to disagree," believing that God can work through each one in spite of or maybe even because of their differences?

_____

_____

_____

_____

_____

_____

_____

8. When churches or individuals are called to different fields of ministry (2:7-9), what can they do to maintain their common connection through Christ, reflecting Paul's remembrance of the poor in Jerusalem (2:10)?

_____

_____

_____

_____

_____

_____

_____

The Church of Two Tables

Galatians 2:11-14

On October 16, 1901, Booker T. Washington dined at the White House as the guest of Theodore Roosevelt. That evening, Washington became the first African American to share the White House table with a president of the United States. On the whole, Roosevelt's racial views were not consistent with "the truth of the gospel" (2:14), but his views were considered progressive in his own day. Roosevelt found his table fellowship with Washington "so natural and so proper."

Late that evening, a reporter routinely checking the White House guest list noticed Washington's name, and at 2:00 a.m. the news hit the wires. African Americans were overjoyed, but a storm of anger, disgust, and condemnation erupted in the South. Roosevelt believed he had done nothing wrong but also realized the political implications of his invitation. Though he wrote to Washington that he "did not care . . . what anybody thought or said about" their dinner, Roosevelt never extended Washington a second invitation to the White House table (Morris, 52-58).

Sharing a meal with a fellow human being is a deeply intimate act. We tend to eat with people we love and cherish (family and friends) and people we value and esteem (clients and colleagues). Table fellowship communicates affirmation and acceptance. Roosevelt's dinner with Washington symbolized an acceptance of African Americans that white Southerners were unwilling to endorse.

The practices of Judaism required by the Missionaries included dietary restrictions and regulations. The Galatians were urged to start a diet that prohibited them from eating certain foods, to prepare foods in certain ways, and to follow certain rules of personal hygiene before pulling up to the table.

Although the law did not specifically forbid the Missionaries from eating with Gentiles, they took no chances. They felt they might inadvertantly violate a rule if they ate with someone who did not share their diet. It was best to eat with one's own people and avoid table fellowship with Gentiles. All Gentiles who converted to their message were expected to do the same.

Sometime after extending the right hand of fellowship to Paul at the Jerusalem council, Peter made an extended visit to Antioch. At the council he rejected the idea that Gentiles must be circumcised before receiving God's grace. In Antioch he affirmed the unity of Jews and Gentiles by eating with his Gentile sisters and brothers. "Then certain people came from James" (2:12) and criticized Peter's choice of dinner companions. Like Roosevelt's response to Southern pressure, Peter's response was to "draw back" and end his table fellowship with Gentiles.

An agreement was reached on Gentile circumcision at the Jerusalem council, but the question of Jews eating with Gentiles was not addressed. Apparently James, and certainly the "circumcision faction," feared a shared table would harm the faith and witness of Jewish Christians. Gentiles did not need to be circumcised or follow the dietary restrictions to receive salvation, but at mealtime (and presumably at the Lord's Supper) Jewish Christians had to maintain their distance from those of a different diet. James apparently had a "separate but equal" view of the church. Jews and Gentiles could belong to the same Christian fellowship but had to eat at separate tables.

The Gospel of One Table

In Galatians, we read that Paul believes if Christ's cross is enough to make people one in salvation, then the cross is enough to make them one at dinner. The cross demolishes the ethnic and religious barriers that separate Jews and Gentiles because those barriers belong to the present evil age. In Christ there is neither Jew nor Gentile but one people (3:28), called into being as witnesses to the new creation. Maintaining two separate tables strengthens and furthers the present evil age. When Jewish and Gentile believers share a common table, God's new creation is on display.

Paul opposes Peter "to his face" (2:11) in a public assembly (2:14) because the stakes are high. Perhaps Peter views his actions as a tactical retreat, preserving his ministry until a more favorable time arrives to show again his true convictions. Paul sees Peter's withdrawal as a denial of the gospel. By conviction, Peter believes Gentiles do not have to become Jews in order to be Christians. But actions speak louder than words, and Peter's withdrawal from table fellowship with Gentiles says faith in Christ is not enough if Gentiles want to join the people of God. Paul speaks up loudly and publicly because Peter is "not acting consistently with the truth of the gospel" (2:14).

Paul and Miss Amy

In 1964, Rev. Vernon Tyson invited the great African American preacher Samuel Proctor to preach at his white church in Sanford, North Carolina. The majority of the church disapproved, and when word of the invitation spread in the community, Tyson received death threats.

The night before Proctor was to preach, Tyson called an emergency meeting of the church board to calm the controversy. The meeting was not going well until a retired teacher rose to speak. She was known as "Miss Amy," and she said,

> "There was a case up near Chapel Hill recently, where a teenage boy went around a curve too fast and was killed in a car crash. So they thought. He was down there by the side of the road and they were just waiting for the ambulance to come and take him to the funeral home. There wasn't any signs of life.
>
> "But then an airman from Pope Air Force Base stopped . . . he scrambled down the embankment and opened that boy's mouth," she continued. "And he saw the man's tongue stuck back in his throat, and he ran his finger back there and pulled out that tongue, and then gave that boy mouth-to-mouth resuscitation. By the time that ambulance got there," Miss Amy said, "that boy was walking around alive as you or me. . . .
>
> "What I haven't told you is that the boy who had the wreck was white, and that airman that saved him was a black man. . . . Now, which one of you fathers would have said to that airman, 'Now don't you run your black fingers down my boy's white throat'? Which of y'all would have told that airman, 'Don't you dare put your black lips on my boy's mouth'?"

Miss Amy sat down, the board voted to support Proctor's visit, and hard hearts began to melt, all because an elderly woman spoke out when her sisters and brothers were living inconsistently with the truth of the gospel (Tyson, 73-81).

Miss Amy's witness reflects Paul's pattern of gospel truth-telling. All the powers of the early church were arrayed against Paul, insisting on the status quo of segregation at the table. Representatives from James, leader of the Jerusalem church, clamped down on Jew-Gentile meal sharing. Peter, certainly not known for bowing to the whims of others, gave in to the pressure and went along with the crowd. Even Barnabas, Paul's trusted colleague in the Gentile mission, counseled patience and concluded the time was not right to go against the system (2:13). Without realizing it, the church gave in to the present evil age.

Someone has to stand up for the truth for the gospel. Someone has to give witness to the new creation. Whenever Christians act inconsistently with the truth of the gospel, the truth of the gospel is at stake. Paul does not mention the outcome of his public stand, but the effectiveness of his rebuke is not the point. What matters is the consistency of his witness, a consistency he prays God will use in persuading the Galatians away from the present evil age.

Life Lessons

Martin Luther King Jr.'s comment that "Sunday morning at 11:00 is the most segregated hour in America" is still true. The more a particular congregation reflects the racial, ethnic, economic, and educational diversity of its community, the more that church reflects the new creation.

While churches seek to create "new creation" diversity in their own fellowship, they can also establish relationships with churches of different backgrounds. Joint services in which churches of different races and ethnic makeup worship together reflect the Spirit's unifying presence (4:6). The meals that often follow create a sense of fellowship that makes us wonder why we cling so strongly to our separate tables.

Because meals are usually smaller and more intimate gatherings, individuals can give powerful witness against the "two-table" system. When businesspeople eat with colleagues of another race on their lunch hour, when soup kitchen volunteers share a meal with the people they serve, when youth groups eat with the people in their school cafeterias with whom no one else will eat, and when families invite people from different backgrounds for a meal in their homes, the new creation claims a little more territory from the present evil age.

If your church has a Wednesday evening meal, I suspect that everyone sits with the same people week after week. When people eat with people they do not know well, they give witness to the new creation. Where church members always eat with the same people, the present evil age has quietly but firmly asserted its influence.

Peter resorted to the two-table system in response to pressure from the "circumcision faction" (2:12). We guard our church and family tables for the same reason. What will people think of us if we go against cultural norms? Peer pressure is real, at the table and in every area of life. We can take comfort however, in the fact that Peter, the great apostle, was not immune to peer pressure. Even Barnabas, called the "son of encouragement" (Acts 4:36), wilted under the circumcision faction's condemning gaze. God is used to working with people who give in to peer pressure, which is good news when we find ourselves seeking human approval.

1. What are some of the barriers preventing people of different backgrounds from eating with each other?

_____

_____

_____

_____

_____

_____

2. What are some examples of a two-table system at work in your community, both today and in the past?

_____

_____

_____

_____

_____

_____

The Church of Two Tables

3. Where is the new creation in view through the work of "one-table" Christians?

_____

_____

_____

_____

_____

_____

4. Has anyone ever been a "Miss Amy" in your life or your church, calling you to act consistently with the truth of the gospel?

_____

_____

_____

_____

_____

5. Could you be a "Miss Amy" for someone else or your church? What is it about such a role that makes us uncomfortable?

_____

_____

_____

_____

_____

_____

6. At what point do we confront people publicly as Paul did? When is it more appropriate to hold sisters and brothers accountable in a private manner?

_____

_____

_____

_____

_____

7. Why is integrating church life to reflect the larger diversity of Christ's followers so difficult?

_____
_____
_____
_____
_____

8. How have you faced peer pressure in the past, and in what areas of your life do you face peer pressure now?

_____
_____
_____
_____
_____

The Church of Two Tables

The Faith of Jesus Christ

Session

Two tiny punctuation marks make an enormous difference in how we understand what Paul says in 2:15-21. The New International Version (NIV) and the New King James Version (NKJV) put 2:15-21 in quotation marks, but the New Revised Standard Version (NRSV) does not. With the quotation marks, the passage continues to be the words Paul spoke publicly to Peter at Antioch. Without the quotation marks, the passage is a direct address to the Galatians that summarizes Paul's argument to this point in the letter.

Several factors argue for including the quotation marks. The phrase "we ourselves are Jews by birth" in 2:15 flows naturally from 2:14 as a reference to Paul, Peter, and the Jewish Christians in Antioch. More importantly, Paul has made his case from personal experiences since 1:11. A summarizing transitional passage separated from his personal story seems out of place. Paul summarizes his argument from within a personal narrative, drawing on a concrete past experience to address present circumstances in Galatia.

Our translation decision directly impacts how we interpret Paul's understanding of justification, the process by which a person becomes righteous. Paul says in 2:16, "we know that a person is justified not by the works of the law but through faith in Jesus Christ." If Paul is making a general statement of theological truth, then the phrase "works of the law" has no referent in a concrete, local situation. It becomes a general phrase referring to any human effort to be justified (become righteous) through one's own merit.

In such a scenario, righteousness is understood in legal terms and is based on how well a person follows a standard of behavior. A judge measures a person's behavior against the standard of law, and if the person's actions meet the standard, the person is justified (declared righteous). Since no one can perfectly meet the standard, Jesus as the sinless suffering servant is judged in our place on the cross, and we are declared righteous as we receive Christ's righteousness by faith.

To everything in the previous sentence, Paul would say, "Amen!" But since 2:16 is part of a sermon directed toward a specific incident in Antioch, Paul approaches justification from a relational instead of a legal perspective in this passage. To be justified/made righteous is to be placed in right relationship with God and with God's people. Sin is more than a failure to meet God's standard of behavior and Jesus' death on the cross does more than help us satisfy a legal code. Sin removes us from right relationship with God and with each other, and Jesus died because God's love for us cannot bear the separation created by our sin.

As part of Paul's sermon, the phrase "works of the law" has a concrete reference point: the disagreement over dietary restrictions in Antioch. When Paul says, "we know that a person is justified not by the works of the law but through faith in Jesus Christ" (2:16), the "we" includes Peter and the Antioch Jewish Christians. Paul, Peter, and the others agree that Gentile Christians are made right with God through Jesus. However, by their refusal of table fellowship with Gentile Christians, Peter and the Antioch Jewish Christians say that Gentile Christians must do the works of the law to be in right relationship with God's people. In Paul's mind, refusing table fellowship is the same as denying Gentile righteousness through Christ, so that at heart Peter and the others still hold the traditional Jewish understanding of Gentiles as "sinners" (2:15).

Paul spells out the implications of Peter's position in 2:17: "But if, in our effort to be justified in Christ, we ourselves have been found to be sinners, is Christ then a servant of sin? Certainly not!" Unlike Peter, Paul boldly dines with Gentile Christians and completely rejects the two-table system. Peter's actions imply that table fellowship with Gentiles makes Paul a sinner, and since Paul's fellowship is done in the name of Jesus, it makes Jesus a servant of sin.

In order to be found a sinner for eating with Gentiles, Paul would have to build up again the very law he has worked so hard to tear down (2:18). By his actions, Peter has done just that, reinstating the distinction the law makes between Jew and Gentile by refusing to eat with his Gentile brothers and sisters. Since this distinction is inconsistent with the truth of the gospel, Peter has sinned according to the gospel while acting righteously according to the law. Paul refuses to build up the law again because he knows he will then become a transgressor by living inconsistently with the truth of the gospel.

The Faith of Jesus Christ

A second translation decision confronts us in 2:16 that once again greatly impacts our interpretation of the passage. The King James Version (KJV) says that a person "is not justified by the works of the law, but by the *faith of* Jesus Christ . . . ." The NIV and the NRSV speak of being justified by and through "*faith in* Christ." Both translations are grammatically correct. The context determines which translation is used.

If Paul uses legal terms in his discussion of justification in this passage, then the "faith in Christ" translation makes better sense. To place one's faith in Christ is the concrete, specific action that transfers Christ's righteousness to the believer. However, since Paul operates from a relational perspective in his Antioch sermon, the "faith of Jesus Christ" translation better reflects the context. The "faith of" Jesus demonstrates God's desire for relationship with sinful human beings. Serving God and people through his life and death, Jesus lived a life of complete faithfulness to God. God the Father raised him from the dead (1:1), vindicating Jesus' faithfulness. Christ's faithfulness overcomes human unfaithfulness and brings sinful people into right relationship with God and each other. Christ's faithfulness also defeats the powers of the present evil age and brings into being the new creation. Human beings give witness to the new creation when their lives reflect the faith of Christ.

Whether translators say "faith in Jesus" or "the faith of Jesus," they agree that Christ is the focal point and that faith is the proper response to Jesus. However, the "faith of" translation places a stronger emphasis on Jesus by focusing on his faith, not ours. The prior *faith of* Jesus creates the possibility of our faith in Jesus. The initiative toward relationship with human beings belongs to God, and the faithfulness of Jesus displays the lengths to which God will go to be in relationship with us.

Jesus Is Everything!

Spontaneous applause erupted after a brilliant performance of Beethoven's Fifth Symphony. The audience stood and cheered as one to show their appreciation. But the conductor, Arturo Toscanini, waved his arms violently for it all to stop. He turned to the orchestra and shouted, "You are nothing!" He pointed to himself and shouted, "I am nothing!" Then he shouted, "Beethoven is everything, everything, everything!" (McCullough, *Trivialization*, 115-16).

To the churches of Galatia, Paul says Jesus is everything, everything, everything! Everything needed to make them right with God and with God's people has already been accomplished through the faithfulness of Christ. Human performance amounts to nothing, unless it is offered in response to Jesus' performance and performed in the power of the Holy Spirit (5:16).

Believing in Christ's faithfulness is the human response that makes a person righteous. Paul says in 2:16, "And we have come to believe in Christ Jesus, so that we might be justified by *the faith of Christ*." We receive the faith of Jesus as we believe in Jesus. By our faith we respond to Jesus' faith, accepting God's invitation to relationship.

By keeping Christ's faith at the forefront, the "faith of Jesus" translation reminds us that our right relationships with God and each other depend on the strength of Jesus' faith, not ours. We are not justified "by the strength or purity of our own believing. If Paul had meant that, then 'faith' would be a new kind of 'work,' a human achievement by which we place ourselves into right relation with God" (Hays, 246). At times our faith is strong and at times weak, but at all times what matters most is Christ's faith.

A New Identity

Jesus' clearest demonstration of faithfulness was on the cross, which means our belief in Jesus is a participation in his faithful death. Paul says, "I have been crucified with Christ" (2:19). Symbolic death with Christ is a death to the law, the source, center, and focus of Paul's "earlier life in Judaism" (1:13). Paul's earlier identity was wrapped up in his ability to keep the law more faithfully than others, earning the approval of his peers and of God, or so Paul thought. The law Paul so zealously defended was an active participant in Jesus' death as we shall see in 3:13, meaning through the law Paul died to the law (2:19). Paul's death to the law contrasts with Peter and the Antioch Jewish Christians and with the Missionaries in Galatia, whose aliveness to the law is on display at every meal.

Paul is now alive to God and given a new identity. No longer does his life revolve around the practices of Judaism and the competition such practices evoked from him. A new source, center, and focus guides Paul's life, so in a symbolic sense he can confess in 2:20, "it is no longer I who live, but it is Christ who lives in me." Jesus does not snatch him away from the present evil age but frees him from it, so that he now lives by *the faith of the Son of God* (2:20). Jesus' faithful death makes possible our faithful life, to the extent that we allow the Holy Spirit to conform our lives to Christ's faithfulness. As Paul's life reflects the faithfulness of Jesus' life, the world will catch a glimpse of the new creation.

A word of caution: Paul's use of "I" language in this section could tempt us to focus on how individuals reflect Christ's faithfulness without reference to the larger body of Christians. Remember that Paul is still responding to personal accusations made against him in Antioch. Paul the individual is accused of making Christ a servant of sin through his table fellowship with Gentiles (2:17). Galatians 2:19-21 concludes Paul's response to these personal charges, making the "I" language necessary. But the "I" language does not change or deemphasize the fact that Paul's individual participation in Christ's death takes place within the community of faith. With his sisters and brothers, Paul has been rescued from the present evil age, and together they (and we) give witness to God's new creation.

Life Lessons

When our first child was born, like most new parents my wife and I found it difficult to keep our house as clean as we once did. We called out for professional help, hiring someone to clean for us. The funny thing was, on the night before the professional arrived, we worked as hard as we always did getting ready for her arrival! We cleared off the kitchen counters, organized the mountains of baby paraphernalia, put away the clothes, and tossed all other loose items into the closet. We cleaned hard so that she could clean.

How often do we act as if the strength of our faith prepares the way for Christ's love to enter our lives? We act as if our faith does the preliminary cleansing, letting Jesus know that we're serious about our need for the deep cleaning only he can give. But faith is not a preliminary work, so the depth of our faith is not the issue. By faith, we allow ourselves to be caught up in the faithful life of Jesus. When the strength of our faith is not on trial, we can rest in the faith that matters most, the faith of Jesus.

1. When you sin and fall short of God's glory, is your first instinct to rush back to God's arms of grace or pull away from God because of the guilt you feel?

_____

_____

_____

_____

_____

_____

2. In what ways do you work hard to clean up your life so that Christ can do the deep cleaning?

_____

_____

_____

_____

_____

_____

3. How does the "faith of Christ" translation strengthen our focus on Jesus?

_____

_____

_____

_____

_____

4. What would you say if asked to describe Jesus' faithfulness to his neighbors and to God?

_____

_____

_____

_____

_____

5. The faith of Jesus puts us in right relationship with each other. How does this change the way we relate with brothers and sisters who have sinned against us?

_____

_____

_____

_____

_____

_____

6. How can the "faith of Christ" translation strengthen our evangelistic efforts?

_____

_____

_____

_____

_____

_____

7. What are some signs that a church or individual is truly living by the faith of Jesus?

_____

_____

_____

_____

_____

_____

8. What other loyalties tempt you to find your identity in something other than Christ?

_____

_____

_____

_____

_____

_____

Paul's report of his sermon at Antioch (2:14-21) concludes the first phase of his argument. His personal narrative rebuts the charges made against him and documents his commitment to a law-free gospel. In Galatians 3 he contends that the Galatians' experience of the Spirit provides further evidence to prove his case (3:1-5). He then appeals to Scripture, saying that the law and the prophets prefigure and support the gospel he preaches.

Bewitched!

Mention the word "bewitched," and many people think of a 1960s television show. A "typical" American housewife just happens to be a witch. She gets herself and her family in and out of trouble with her magic. With a quick wiggle of her nose, people are "bewitched," doing and saying things they would never do of their own accord.

After calling them foolish, Paul asks the Galatians, "Who has bewitched you?" (3:1). As in our day, people in the ancient world associated the word "bewitched" with magic. Paul wonders if the Missionaries have cast a spell over the Galatians to get them interested in a law-based message. Since Paul had proclaimed the crucified Christ in their midst, the Galatians should know better than to listen to the Missionaries. Paul struggles to understand the Galatians' alarming interest in a perversion of the gospel, an interest so strange that it might be attributable to magic.

The strangest aspect of the Galatians' behavior is their interest in the law *after* they have already received the Spirit. Paul asks a rhetorical question: "Did you receive the Spirit by doing the works of the law or by believing what you heard?" (3:2). The obvious answer: they received the Spirit when they believed the message about Christ's faithfulness.

Perhaps the Missionaries have "bewitched" the Galatians in a non-magical way. It seems the Missionaries are suggesting that once the Spirit is received through Christ, the law is necessary to bring a person's life to the perfection expected by God. Specific guidelines are needed to show the Gentiles how to follow Jesus. A checklist of things to do is necessary to help them mature in the faith. The Spirit may work miracles among them (3:5), but the law is needed to lead them in the ways of God's people.

Paul recognizes immediately the foolishness of adding the law to the Spirit. "Are you so foolish?" he asks the Galatians in 3:3. "Having started with the Spirit, are you now ending with the flesh?" If they look to the law for guidance, the Galatians will live out their God-initiated, Spirit-filled lives in Christ by relying on their own strength (their flesh). They will in effect say, "God started us along this journey but we'll take it from here and finish the job."

The myth of independence and self-reliance, wrapped up in the Missionaries' law-based message, is in the process of bewitching the Galatians. Paul hopes his letter is not too late to turn the tide (3:4).

The Descendants of Abraham

Paul appeals to Abraham, the "father" of Israel, to show the Galatians that they are already part of God's family. No doubt the Missionaries offered Abraham's obedience in support of their cause. In Genesis 17, God commands Abraham to be circumcised, and Abraham obeys. Following from this, a natural argument for the Missionaries would have been that Gentiles should be circumcised because Abraham was circumcised. But Paul quotes Genesis 15, which says that Abraham "believed God, and it was reckoned to him as righteousness" (Gal 3:6). Before Abraham is circumcised in Genesis 17, Genesis 15 calls him righteous because of his faith. Faith comes first, then obedience that reflects the right relationships received through faith.

Abraham's faith does not move God to action. God evokes faith from Abraham by making promises. God promises to make a great nation out of Abraham and Sarah's family. God promises them many descendants and a land to call their own. Abraham believes God will be faithful to these promises, and because of this trust he is called righteous. Before Abraham obeys and even before he believes, God's faithfulness is at work.

People who believed in God's faithfulness to Israel in the time before Christ's advent and people who now believe in the faithfulness of Jesus are the descendants of Abraham. Jew or Gentile, what matters most is believing (like Abraham) in the faithfulness of God. The Missionaries urged the Gentile Galatians to add the practices of Judaism to their faith so that they could become Abraham's descendants. Paul in effect told the Galatian Christians, "Don't bother! You're already part of Abraham's family."

God's Unchanging Plan

God planned to include Gentiles in the family from the beginning. Paul says, "And the scripture, foreseeing that God would justify the Gentiles by faith, declared the gospel beforehand to Abraham, saying, 'All the Gentiles shall be blessed in you'" (3:8). He bases the quotation on Genesis 12:3, which contains God's original promises to Abraham. God promises to make a great nation out of Abraham and Sarah's descendants not for their own benefit, but in order to bless the entire world. Through the faithfulness of Jesus Christ, God makes good on the promise to bless the Gentiles.

The vision of a faith-based Gentile mission is rooted in Scripture, not Paul's imagination. Preaching the law-free gospel to Gentiles "is not just Paul's pet project, a decision to widen the mission the way a business enlarges by setting up branch offices. It has been a part of God's intention from the beginning, explicit in the call to Abraham" (Cousar, 73). Paul lifts up the Gentiles; they have been on God's mind from the start.

Sticking to Paul's Argument

As we move from Abraham's story to the law's story (3:10-14), we enter one of the most difficult passages to interpret in all of Paul's letters. When we see this passage as an abstract theological statement, we produce doctrines that may be true but that are not true to Paul's original intent. Remembering that all of Galatians is part of Paul's argument against the Missionaries is the best way to make it through any interpretive challenges.

The dominant Protestant interpretation views 3:10-14 as a systematic statement on human sinfulness, guilt before God, and salvation through Christ. The law pronounces a curse on all who fail to keep its precepts. Since the law cannot be perfectly obeyed, it reveals the impossibility of earning righteousness through human merit. Jesus Christ perfectly kept the law, became a curse for us on the cross, and redeemed us in the process. We receive Christ's redemption through faith.

A different focus emerges if we situate 3:10-14 within Paul's argument against the Missionaries. Paul wants to show how Gentiles are now part of God's family apart from the law, so a general statement on salvation is not his aim. The passage is one part of a high-stakes argument between rival groups of Jewish Christians. Paul dives into the law to prove that Christ has ended the law's reign and established the law-free new creation, where Jew and Gentile live in right relationship with God and with each other.

A New, New Identity?

Having argued that their faith in the faithfulness of Jesus makes them descendants of Abraham, Paul now warns the Galatians what they will get themselves into if they embrace the Missionaries' law-based message. To embrace the law is to embrace a part of God's plan not meant for them. They will turn away from the new creation and enter again the present evil age, which Paul characterizes as life under a curse.

"For all who rely on the works of the law are under a curse," Paul states at the beginning of 3:10. The key word in this phrase is "rely." The Galatians relied on the Spirit when their life in Christ began (3:3), but the Missionaries have told them to rely on their own ability to keep the law. The Galatians want to trade the identity they received through Christ's gift of faithfulness for an identity based on law observance.

Imagine you are the proud owner of a mountain cottage. The most striking feature of your cottage is a gigantic window through which you can see the mountains in all their glory. Night and day, you gaze through that window and marvel at the beauty of it all.

But soon you notice some smudges on the window. You quickly clean the dirty spots and resume your watch. Then you notice your window attracts the attention of birds that leave their calling cards, so you pull out a ladder and start scrubbing. Friends with dirty-fingered children stop by to visit, and before their van pulls out of your driveway, the buckets are out and you start cleaning. You are amazed at how quickly your beautiful window becomes dirty, and you buy all manner of cleaning supplies in response. As a result of your efforts you have the cleanest window in the mountains, but you no longer take time to enjoy the view (Peterson).

The Missionaries, like many of their ancestors in Israel, give great attention to keeping the window clean but never see the beauty beyond the window. They devote their energy to keeping the law and lose sight of the God to whom the law points. They locate their identity in law-observance instead of God's promises fulfilled in Christ, and they want the Galatians to do the same.

The Curse of Exile

At the end of 3:10, Paul quotes from Deuteronomy 27:26, saying, "Cursed is everyone who does not observe and obey all the things written in the book of the law." Within the context of Deuteronomy 27 and 28, the curse to which Paul refers is corporate instead of individual. God identifies the corporate blessings that will come to Israel if the nation obeys the law, as well as the corporate curses that will come if they disobey.

The curses of Deuteronomy 27 and 28 can be summarized in one word: exile. Obedience and blessing lie within the realm of possibility for the Israelites. But even as he gives the law from God, Moses knows which way the people will go. He says in Deuteronomy 31:29, "For I know that after my death you will surely act corruptly, turning aside from the way that I have commanded you. In time to come trouble will befall you, because you will do what is evil in the sight of the LORD, provoking him to anger through the work of your hands." Moses' prediction comes true—the Israelites disobey, and calamity follows. First the Assyrians, then the Babylonians, the Persians, and finally the Romans conquer Israel. The Babylonians march the Israelites into exile, and even though they had returned home by the time of Jesus, as long as Herod was on the throne the curse of exile continued.

The structure of the law may sound appealing. The security of belonging to an exclusive group where the boundaries between insider and outsider are clear might be a plus. A system in which one can advance beyond one's peers surely excited the competitive juices of more than a few Galatians. But in gaining these things, the Gentile Galatians would also have taken on Israel's defeat, slavery, and exile under the law's curse. Even if the Galatians matched Paul's earlier law observance and could say of themselves as Paul does, "as to righteousness under the law, blameless" (Phil 3:6), they still could not achieve the life they were created to live—the life of right relationship with God and with each other.

Live by Faith

The law simply cannot produce right relationships because it was never intended to do so. Making relationships right was, is, and always will be a function of faith: God's faithfulness and our response of faith. In 3:11 Paul quotes Habakkuk 2:4, saying, "The one who is righteous will live by faith." The prophet Habakkuk witnessed firsthand the destruction of Israel as a result of the people's disobedience. Faced with the reality of the curse, Habakkuk's word from the Lord is a word of faith. The prophet pointed people back to the promise Abraham received from God's faithfulness and to Abraham's response of faith. Just as Abraham received right relationship with God through faith, so all who would be justified must do the same.

In 3:12 Paul returns to the "prediction of exile" theme in the law. He quotes Leviticus 18:5, which says, "Whoever does the works of the law will live by them." The verse mirrors Deuteronomy 27–28, commanding the Israelites to do certain things in order to live in the promised land. If they disobey, God says, "I will set my face against you, and you shall be struck down by your enemies; your foes shall rule over you, and you shall flee though no one pursues you" (Lev 26:17). The law rested on Israel's works, Israel failed to obey, and exile was the result.

While the Leviticus quotation strengthens Paul's reference to the curse of exile, it also "simply asserts that the Torah *as it stands* is not the means of faith, since it speaks of 'doing'" (Wright, 150) and not trusting in the promise. The law asks something different of Israel than the promise, and the promise is of far greater importance. Because the law does not rest on faith, it cannot bring a person into right relationship with God and with God's people.

Redemption

Paul's journey through the law and the prophets leads him to Deuteronomy 21:23, where he finds the cross: "Cursed is everyone who hangs on a tree." A dead man hanging on a tree brings a curse, but in God's hands the dead Jesus on the cross redeemed Israel from the curse of the law. Israel's sin and Jesus as Israel's fully obedient representative and Messiah took on himself the weight of the world's sin. He became the curse, carried the curse to the grave, and buried it there. The resurrection brought the end of the curse, new life to Israel, and a new day for the Gentiles.

Because Jesus became a curse, the law's curse of exile is not the final word for Israel. "Christ redeemed us from the curse of the law," Paul says in 3:13. The word "redeemed" describes freedom from slavery, which means that Jesus set Israel free from slavery to the law and the curse it pronounced on her disobedience. Through his faithfulness, Jesus delivered the Israelites from exile and welcomed them home as God's people. "Home" is not a place on the political map where Israel can once again be a sovereign nation; the Romans still rule. "Home" is the new creation where Israel can finally be all that God calls her to be, the new Israel where Jew and Gentile alike live in right relationship with God and with each other.

The World Is Blessed

In 3:14 Paul mentions Abraham again, referring to the blessing his descendants would bring to the Gentiles (3:8). Choosing not to live by the promise, Israel disobeyed the law and became sidetracked from its original mission of worldwide blessing. Through Jesus, Israel can now be the blessing God promised she would be, and Paul is an agent of that blessing as he preaches to the Gentiles. The sign that the curse is over and the blessing available to all is on display in Galatia. The Gentiles have received the Spirit through the faithfulness of Jesus.

Life Lessons

In Wendell Berry's novel *Jayber Crow*, a small-town barber retires to a riverside cabin just outside of town. Expecting to spend his time fishing and gardening, Jayber Crow soon finds himself cutting hair again when his faithful customers find their way to the cabin. He realizes that their coming is "an act of faith because in this house on the river I have no mirrors on the walls. . . . When they climb into the chair, they have to trust me" (Berry, 306).

We cannot see God, and at times what we see in this world makes us wonder if the new creation really exists. We cannot always see what God is doing in our lives. At such times we resist the urge to take control, we stay in the chair, and we trust. Like Abraham, we believe the promises will come true. Like Habakkuk, we proclaim that the righteous will live by faith. Like Jesus, we place ourselves in God's hands, not our own.

At its core, Christian faith involves trusting the God who makes and keeps promises. The life of discipleship cannot revolve around keeping rules, whether the law of Israel or the checklists we devise to define what a good Christian should be and do. Rule-keeping leads to the exile of self-dependence, where trust in God is diminished. True life, life as God created it to be lived, happens when people embrace their dependence on God.

1. In what ways do we say to God, "I'll take care of things from here," and try to chart, plan, and implement our own spiritual growth?

_____
_____
_____
_____
_____

2. What are the ideas and temptations that "bewitch" churches and individual believers today?

_____
_____
_____
_____
_____

3. Why is the myth of self-reliance so appealing?

_____
_____
_____
_____
_____

4. What are some signs that we are "cleaning the window" with our spiritual disciplines instead of looking through it to see God?

_____
_____
_____
_____
_____

5. What made living a life governed by the law desirable to the Galatians? What makes it so for us?

_____

_____

_____

_____

_____

_____

6. How did Israelite dependence on the law obstruct Israel's call to be a blessing to the nations?

_____

_____

_____

_____

_____

_____

7. What are the obstacles we face to deepening our trust in God?

_____

_____

_____

_____

_____

_____

8. Who are the people you know who have deep trust in God? In what ways is their trust demonstrated?

_____

_____

_____

_____

_____

_____

The Supremacy of Faith

Promise Fulfilled

Galatians 3:15-29

The University of North Carolina and the University of Georgia have an ongoing feud that cannot be settled in the classroom or on the athletic fields. Both claim to be the first public university in the United States of America. UGA was the first public university to receive its charter, but UNC was the first public university to hold classes. How you answer the question depends on how you define the founding of a university.

To a person unaffiliated with either school, the feud might seem inconsequential, even ridiculous. But in actuality, much is at stake. Being the first to begin any new endeavor often grants priority in determining the nature of that endeavor. The first public university can lay claim to being the trendsetter, visionary, and foundation of what has become an enormous educational system.

Four hundred and thirty years after Abraham believed God's promises (3:17), Israel received the law. God delivered the Israelites from slavery in Egypt, led them to the promised land, and along the way gave a law that defines how people who believe God's promises should live. This law has a specific role (3:19-25), but its role is conditioned by the promise. The promise shapes, determines, and guides how the law is understood.

Since the promise has priority, the law does not have the power to annul or add to the promises made to Abraham (3:15). If a second party asks the judge to add to or annul a person's will without that person's permission, the petition will be thrown out of court. By their actions, many Israelites acted as if the law had added to or even annulled the promise, but God ruled them out of order and threw out the law through the faithfulness of Jesus.

The offspring, or seed, of Abraham that God used to fulfill the promises was not law-observant Israel, but Christ. Paul interprets the word "seed" as singular instead of plural. The inheritance of Abraham, that of being part of God's family, comes to us not through keeping the law but through God's promise to Abraham, now fulfilled in Jesus.

Why Then the Law?

The Galatians may have been wondering at this point, "Is there any value in the law?" If the law is as bad as Paul says it is, then why did God bother giving it in the first place? Paul's answer: "It was added because of transgressions" (3:19). The law enables people to name and identify their sins. Through the course of human development, a general knowledge of right and wrong can naturally arise, but the knowledge of how our wrong actions break our fellowship with God and each other cannot be gained through human effort. God reveals that our wrong actions are actually *sins*, establishing a theological category to define human misdeeds. In the process of naming our *sins* God reveals our *sinfulness*, our inability to eradicate sin from our lives. As God's representative people in the world, the Israelites receive the law so that sin can be named in their midst, and hopefully restrained in the process. Human begins must be taught that we are sinners. Through Israel all people learn of their sinful nature.

After exhaustive efforts to show the law's inferiority to the promise, Paul must now show that the law is not opposed to the promises (3:21). The law does not compete with the promises but prepares for their fulfillment through the naming of sins. The law can be misused, however, as in the current Galatian crisis. Trouble arises when people ask the law to do what it cannot do: make them alive to God and to each other through the establishment of right relationships. The law names sins but cannot prevent people from sinning; it identifies but cannot defeat sin's power.

Empowered to name but impotent to save, the law functions as a prison, keeping Israel within its walls until the time for God's decisive defeat of sin arrives (3:22-23). Prison imagery communicates the helpless nature of the human plight. We cannot escape imprisonment to sin through our own efforts, and within this prison we cannot live as God created us to live. Through the law the Israelites learn that they and all people are in bondage to sin, imprisoned and guarded and with no means to escape. "In such a desperate situation, the only hope is for God to act" (Hays, 269). By naming human hopelessness from within the prison of sin, the law rightly used sends people in search of God. In the promise to Abraham, they find evidence of God's faithfulness. In the faithfulness of Jesus, they find God's promises fulfilled and freedom from prison granted.

The law also functions as a disciplinarian (3:24). Paul has in mind the ancient practice of assigning a slave to watch over the master's boy. The slave does not educate the boy, but guards, supervises, and restrains the boy so that he can make it safely to adulthood. Through naming and restraining sin, the law guards and escorts Israel during the time before Jew and Gentile can be justified through the faith of Jesus.

Inferior and Temporary

While defining the law's valuable role in the coming of faith, Paul maintains his emphasis on the law's inferiority to the promise and its fulfillment. At the end of 3:19, he refers to angels and a mediator in describing how Israel received the law. Exodus 19 does not mention the presence of angels at Mount Sinai when God gives the law, but it does describe in vivid detail the lightning, clouds, and fire that accompanied the event. Such natural occurrences were associated with angels in ancient days, and Deuteronomy 33:2 reflects this association as Moses remembers the event: "The LORD came from Sinai . . . . With him were myriads of holy ones; at his right, a host of his own." The mediator at Sinai was Moses, who mediated between two parties, the Israelites and God (3:20).

Paul seems to be saying that God gave the law indirectly, working through angels and Moses the mediator. In contrast, God gave the promises directly to Abraham and God fulfills the promises directly through Jesus. Because the promises given and fulfilled are direct acts of God, they are superior to the indirectly given law.

Inferior to the promises, the law's functions are needed only temporarily. The naming and restraining purpose is to last "until the offspring would come to whom the promise had been made" (3:19). The law's function of naming sin's imprisoning power occurs "so that what was promised through *the faith of Jesus Christ* might be given to those who believe" (3:21). The law's period as guardian was to last "until faith would be revealed" (3:22). Once the faith of Jesus arrives, there is no need for a disciplinarian (3:25). The Galatians want to come under a law that has already fulfilled its purpose. Paul stands at the gate of the prison they are about to enter and says, "Don't go in! Jesus Christ has already set you free!"

One Family

After showing how the law names and restrains sin and how Jesus sets us free from imprisonment to sin, Paul celebrates God's creation of one family through Jesus (3:26-29). If he were writing an abstract systematic statement about personal salvation, we would expect a celebration of individual freedom at this point. But since he is writing a specific appeal to a community divided into two families, he shows how the law's purpose and Jesus' fulfillment of the promise brings those two families together as one.

Everyone who believes in the faithfulness of Jesus receives the title *son* or *daughter of God,* "for in Christ Jesus you are all children of God through faith" (3:26). In the Old Testament, "sons" or "children" of God referred specifically to the Israelites and communicated their status as God's chosen people. As members of the same family through Christ, Gentiles now join their Jewish Christian sisters and brothers and go by the name *child of God.*

Circumcision no longer marks one's membership in God's family; baptism does (3:27). The Missionaries think the Galatians are not full members of the family until they embrace circumcision. Paul says they received God's full family embrace when they were baptized.

In God's one family, our identity is determined by our oneness in Jesus and not by any human distinction. Paul writes, "There is no longer Jew or Greek, there is no longer slave or free, there is no longer male and female; for all of you are one in Christ Jesus" (3:28). The Jew/Gentile distinction created by the law and perpetuated by Peter in Antioch and the Missionaries in Galatia no longer matters in Christ. In God's new creation, all social distinctions fall by the wayside. People are one with each other regardless of ethnicity, economic status, gender, or any other form of human classification. People do not cease being Jews, Gentiles, slaves, free people, men, or women when they receive Christ, but these characteristics no longer determine their identity and can no longer be used to include or exclude them from or within God's family.

Our identity becomes wrapped up in Jesus, not our own accomplishments. As Ellen Charry states, "Unity in Christ marginalizes other dimensions of identity. . . . Subordination of biological and cultural identity to God's work in Christ redirects attention from self to God" (38).

God's goal of one human family was stated clearly in the original promises to Abraham. Jesus Christ accomplished the goal, bringing Jew and Gentile into God's family by faith. To Jew and Gentile alike, Paul says, "if you belong to Christ, then you are Abraham's offspring, heirs according to the promise" (3:29).

The New Creation in View

God created Israel through Abraham's family so that the world could be blessed. In the same way, God creates one family through Jesus so that the world can see the reality of God's new creation. When ethnic, economic, and gender distinctions are used to exclude some and elevate others, the influence of the present evil age is at work. When people are valued equally in Christ and honored consistently as God's children regardless of these human distinctions, the new creation is on display.

Paul says that through baptism we are clothed with Christ (3:27). In baptism we clothe ourselves with Christ's characteristics, and through the Holy Spirit those characteristics become part of who we are. Only as a community of individuals clothed in Christ and living by the Spirit can the church experience oneness in Christ. This experience is vital not just for the church itself but also for the world. A local church clothed with Christ and exhibiting oneness in Christ gives witness to the world of God's new creation in Christ.

Life Lessons

The ability to name our sins is a great gift. The more knowledge we have of our own specific patterns of sinfulness, the more we see how far short we fall of God's design for human relationships. Instead of leading us to despair, such knowledge increases our dependence on God. Knowledge of sin combats our tendency to think more highly of ourselves than we ought and anchors our trust in God.

Knowledge of our own sinfulness is crucial if we are to experience, embrace, and give witness to the way Jesus gathers people of all human backgrounds and makes them one through his faithfulness. Instead of seeing a person based on the color of their skin, the sound of their accent, or the size of their bank account, we see all people as fellow sinners who are as dependent on God's grace as we are.

Out of this group of redeemed sinners, God calls some people to positions of ordained leadership. Racial (Jew or Gentile), economic (slave or free), and gender (male and female) distinctions are no longer the primary factors in determining relationships within the church since we are all one in Christ. Therefore, the question of who can serve as our pastors has nothing to do with race, economic status, or gender, and everything to do with God's call.

If we are to read Paul's letter to the Galatians within the larger context and spirit of the New Testament, we find that an ordained woman proclaiming the gospel of Christ as pastor of a church has nothing to do with political correctness or progressive social views. The presence of female pastors shows that the gospel really does transform human relationships and in the process gives witness to the new creation.

1. What were some of your earliest understandings of sin? Did what you were taught about sin lead you to joyfully embrace God's grace or just make you feel guilty?

_____

_____

_____

_____

_____

_____

2. How should we teach children that they are sinners?

_____

_____

_____

_____

_____

_____

3. How do we teach an unchurched, morally upright person that he or she is a sinner?

_____

_____

_____

_____

_____

4. In what ways is sin an imprisoning power in the world and in our lives?

_____
_____
_____
_____
_____

5. Through Jesus we become children of God, and God says of us, "You are my son/daughter, my beloved." We believe in our minds that we are God's beloved children, but why is it often so hard for this knowledge to move from our minds to our hearts?

_____
_____
_____
_____
_____
_____

6. How is baptism a "clothing" process?

_____
_____
_____
_____
_____
_____

7. What are some of the human distinctions we are tempted to maintain in the church, even though Christ has made us all one?

_____
_____
_____
_____
_____
_____

Promise Fulfilled

8. Describe a time when you experienced the oneness in Christ that transcends racial and cultural divides.

_____

_____

_____

_____

_____

_____

Freed Slaves, Adopted Children, and Friends

Galatians 4:1-20

"All people are enslaved to something." While not an exact quote, the preceding sentence captures in essence what Paul says at the beginning of Galatians 4. Human beings may think they control their own destinies and chart their own paths. We may believe we have complete autonomy in our choices and decisions. But Paul says there are forces at work in the world that enslave us and prevent us from living the lives we were created to live.

The good news of the gospel is that the enslaving forces of the present evil age are no match for the One who gave himself for our sins (1:4). Jesus sets us free so that we can "through love become slaves to one another" (5:13), thus fulfilling our created purpose. When Jesus sets us free, he gives us a new family in which to lose and live our lives.

Minors, Slaves, and the Stoicheia

Paul refers to "heirs according to the promise" in 3:29, then switches to heirs according to birth order to make his next point. In Paul's patriarchal society, the first male heir received his father's property at "a date set by the father" (4:2). Yet while he was a minor, the heir was no better than a slave (4:1). Guardians and trustees made the major decisions even though the heir would one day be the owner. The heir was in a much better position than the slave, so "the similarity between the minor and the slave is one of appearance only. The point Paul wants to make is, however, clear: both, the minor and the slave, lack the capacity of self-determination" (Betz, 203).

Paul applies the heir/minor imagery to Jews and Gentiles since both were enslaved to the "elemental spirits" (4:3, 9) until the "date set by the father," when Christ set them free. A consensus among scholars as to what Paul means by "elemental spirits" is hard to reach. Hays lists three possible translations and interpretations of the Greek word *stoicheia* (282):

• "elemental principles," the basic principles of any field of knowledge.
• the "elemental substances" of earth, air, fire, and water.
• "elemental spirits," as in "the spiritual forces of evil in the heavenly places" from Eph 6:4.

In the absence of consensus, perhaps the best approach is to draw from all three interpretations. "Elemental substances" played a large role in the "pagan" religions the Galatians embraced before receiving the faith of Jesus. The elements of the universe, including earth, air, fire, water, and particularly the stars, were objects of worship. "Elemental principles" applies to the basic principles of religion, whether pagan religions or Israelite religion. "Elemental spirits" enslave by invading and distorting the substances and principles of Jewish and pagan religions.

Paul does not say that the Jewish and pagan religions originated with the elemental spirits. Before they knew Jesus, the Gentiles developed pagan religions as part of their God-given time to "search for God" (Acts 17:27). Luke tells us in Acts 17:30 that God overlooked this time of ignorance, suggesting the development of these religions was not the direct work of the demonic but a natural human process. In the case of Israel, Paul obviously believes the faith of Israel began with God's direct promise to Abraham, without any influence from "elemental spirits."

The "elemental spirits" enslave Gentiles by using the "elemental substances" of pagan religions to lead people away from God instead of to God. These same spirits distort the "elemental principles" of Israelite faith, enslaving people to law-observance instead of freeing them to live in light of God's promises. In both cases, the demonic forces twist an effort to know God into a rule-based human exercise in religion. The enslavement occurs when people view their religious observances as ends in themselves, instead of means through which they become aware of God's presence. Instead of preparing them to receive the gospel Paul proclaims, the pagan religions (under the influence of the elemental spirits) focused the Gentiles on "beings that by nature are not gods" (4:8). Instead of keeping them glued to the promises, the law (under the influence of the elemental spirits) distracted the Israelites away from God and kept their focus on following the rules.

Paul argues that enslaving elemental spirits are part of what makes this a present evil age. In 4:3 he identifies the corporate work of these spirits as they inhabit not individuals, but the religions of both Gentiles and Jews. Paul does not say that some outside force dictates and determines our every move. Instead, he argues that demonic forces invade, influence, and shape the larger systems that shape our lives. Whether the systems are cultural, economic, governmental, or religious (see Session 1), these systems shape our thoughts, habits, and patterns of living. Because elemental spirits shape the larger systems that shape us, Paul says that enslavement is the universal human condition.

The Fullness of Time

People in bondage require deliverance. Escape is not possible. An outside force must invade and set the captives free. "But when the fullness of time had come, God sent his Son" (4:4), and the invasion commenced. Paul highlights the cross and resurrection when he says Jesus set us free from the present evil age (1:1-4); now he offers another angle on the same liberating story by focusing on the incarnation. At "the date set by the father" (4:2), God sent Jesus into the world to set us free. Instead of a gradual process through which freedom from the elemental spirits was achieved, God launched a direct assault on all that enslaves human beings, and defeated these powers decisively.

Jesus was "born of a woman, born under the law" (4:4), which is another way of saying he was fully human and fully Jewish. God's invasion took place from within a particular people who were chosen by God to bless the world, yet lived under the law's curse. Jesus redeemed "those who were under the law" (4:5), ending the curse of exile and setting Israel free to bless the nations. Through Jesus the Gentiles were adopted into God's one new family, composed of Jewish and Gentile believers. These believers were placed in a web of relationships in which everyone is either a sister or brother. Along with a new parent, each adopted person receives a host of new siblings.

The Spirit's presence animates and unites God's new family. The same Spirit lives in each family member, whether Jew or Gentile, binding them together within the presence of God. In excluding Gentile believers from their tables, the two-table party in

Antioch excluded people in whom the Spirit of God dwells. By insisting that the Galatians embrace the practices of Judaism, the Missionaries say the Spirit's presence in a person is not enough to make that person "family."

The Spirit Cries "Abba!"

Readers of the New Testament are familiar with the cry, "Abba! Father!" Jesus used this intensely personal form of address in Gethsemane as he asked God "to remove this cup from me; yet not what I want, but what you want" (Mark 14:36). In Romans 8:15-16, Paul says that through the Spirit we make the same cry to God and so give witness to our adoption as God's children. In Galatians 4:6, however, Paul says that *the Spirit* makes the cry from within us. In a letter that gives priority to Christ's faith before human faith, it is not surprising that Paul emphasizes the Spirit's cry and not our own. Through the Spirit, God does much more than guide and empower believers. The Spirit's cry confirms the individual believer's inclusion in God's family, bringing each person into a conversation between the Spirit and the Father and Son.

Why Turn Back?

"Pour out your anger on the nations that do not know you," the psalmist cries out to God. Psalm 79:6 articulates the common Israelite assumption that the Gentiles do not know God and cannot know God unless they become a part of Israel, the people of God. Paul relies on this background assumption in 4:8, speaking of the time when the Galatians did not know God. It was a time of enslavement; the elemental spirits used the Gentile system of pagan gods to turn people away from the one true God instead of preparing them to receive God's messenger (Paul) and God's Son.

Jesus Christ broke into the Gentiles' prison, opened their ears to Paul's proclamation, and opened their hearts to the gospel. Because of Christ's invasion, Paul writes in 4:9, the Galatians "have come to know God." By receiving the liberating knowledge of Christ's faithfulness, the Galatians now have knowledge of the God for whom they and their ancestors have been searching throughout all their days of pagan worship. But those days of pagan worship, shaped as they were by the elemental spirits, still retain their influence. The idea that God can be found if human beings strive hard enough dies hard. So Paul clarifies himself, saying the Galatians have not come to know God on their own; they have come "to be known by God." The initiative rests with God, the first move is God's move, and the catalyst is not human striving but God's self-revealing. Through Jesus God seeks to know (live in relationship with) the Gentiles. Gentiles come to know God as they respond to God's desire to be known.

The implicit question of the entire letter is made explicit when Paul exclaims, "How can you turn again to the weak and beggarly elemental spirits?" The embrace of Judaism equals a return to paganism, not because the two forms of religion are identical but because both have come under the power of the elemental spirits. These demonic forces focus Jews and Gentiles on the practices of their religion and not the object of their faith. Rightly understood, the Jewish calendar of special days, months, seasons, and years sharpens attentiveness to God. But the Missionaries use the calendar to prove their faithfulness and make a name for themselves among their peers. The Gentiles did the same things through the astronomically-based calendars of pagan religions, but turned their calendars in when they met Jesus. In all likelihood the Missionaries have put forth the Jewish calendar as the one true calendar. In reality the Missionaries are selling back the calendar the Gentiles have already exchanged.

The elemental spirits that enslave Jew and Gentile alike are "weak and beggarly." They have the power to enslave human beings, but they are no match for the power of Christ, who makes beggars of these spirits through his life, death, and resurrection. These "demonic forces hold in thrall the minds of men and women who follow their dictates, but lose their potency as soon as those minds are emancipated in Christ" (Bruce, 202). Formerly in thrall to demonic forces that, like the Jewish law (3:21), could not make them fully alive in relation with God and each other, the Galatians now consider a voluntary return to the spirits that once enslaved them.

Why would anyone exchange freedom for slavery, especially after one had tasted true liberation? Freedom demands responsibility from those to whom it is given. While Paul surely gave attention to basic questions of discipleship once the Galatians received the faith of Jesus, his primary exhortation most likely was to rely on the Spirit (5:16-26). Instead of relying on themselves or on an authority figure or document, the Galatians are to trust God.

Authoritative leaders and structures often provide security and stability for people who would rather have someone else do the hard thinking and hard work that life requires. It is easier to exchange the responsibility of freedom for a slavery in which someone else is responsible. The Missionaries "offered the security of the law, a clear way to order life and measure one's status and success with the religious group" (Baker, 91). Instead of following the Spirit wherever the Spirit leads, the Galatians are tempted to follow the law, with its predictable and measurable requirements. If the Galatians exchange the freedom of life lived in right relationship with God and with God's people for a life of slavery to a non-relational law, Paul's work among them will be wasted (4:11).

What Happened to Our Friendship?

When friends resist our efforts to influence their direction or thinking, we often appeal to the friendship itself. Where reasoned arguments fail to change minds, we hope that personal loyalty will produce the desired results. Paul makes such an appeal in 4:12-20.

The great irony of the situation is that Paul the Jew became like a Gentile when he was with the Galatians, and now the Galatian Gentiles want to become like Jews. No two-table system emerged through Paul's ministry among them, and the practices of Judaism were not included in Paul's proclamation. While in Galatia, Paul lived out his conviction that in Christ, Jews and Gentiles are part of one family. He erected no barriers between himself and his Gentile sisters and brothers. In 4:12 Paul begs the Galatians to become like him in his law-free understanding of the gospel.

That Paul must "beg" the Galatians to follow his example displays both the gravity of the situation and the depth of connection he feels with them. Their connection originated with the Galatians' hospitality, not with Paul's service to them. Paul was passing through the area on the way elsewhere when an illness forced him to stop and stay (4:13). His illness is unknown, but the Galatians' care for him while he is sick is clear. His condition tested their hospitality, and they passed with flying colors. After showing compassion for Paul in his weakness, they responded to the compassion of Christ as proclaimed in Paul's preaching. Paul says, "had it been possible, you would have torn out your eyes and given them to me" (4:15), which is the ancient equivalent of our own saying, "I'd give you my right arm if I could." Clearly the connection is close, and if Paul has not convinced them through reasoned argument thus far, perhaps the appeal to friendship will stir an opening in Galatian hearts.

The depth of their friendship makes the possibility of Galatian betrayal all the more confusing and alarming. "Have I now become your enemy by telling you the truth?" Paul asks in 4:16. Only an outside influence could create such a reversal. The Galatians have not changed their minds about Paul after further reflection on his character and message. In the process of confusing the Galatians with a perversion of the gospel (1:7), the Missionaries poison their personal feelings toward Paul.

The source of Paul's new status as enemy appears to be the law-free gospel he proclaims "by telling the truth." The Missionaries claim that Paul has only given the partial truth, deliberately with-holding the truth of the law so that the Galatians will embrace him (1:10). We can imagine the Missionaries asking, "How can you trust someone who knowingly withholds something so important?" Having trusted Paul with their lives and embraced him as friend, the Galatians apparently feel victimized and taken advantage of when they hear the "rest of the story."

The Missionaries do more than simply "fill in the blanks" they say Paul left open. Their approach to the Galatians is more subtle and calculating. "They make much of you" (4:16), Paul says to his friends. The image is one of courtship, and the implication is that of flirting and flattering. But the flattery has a rough edge. The Missionaries shower the Galatians with attention not to make the Galatians feel good about themselves, but to influence the Galatians to become like the Missionaries. The Galatians receive an excluding message made appealing by its soothing tone, perhaps sounding like this: "You're too good to follow someone like Paul. Let us show you what God's people are really about. Do what we tell you and you'll be 'in.'"

Paul sees through the flattery and knows the Missionaries want to make a name for themselves by "stealing" converts from the apos-tle to the Gentiles. Paul says he "courted" them in the right way, not for his own sake but out of true love for the Galatians. "It is good to be made much of for a good purpose at all times, and not only when I am present with you" (4:18). Paul made much of the Galatians during his visits and is still making much of them through his letter. The angry tone communicates how much the Galatians matter to Paul. He cares enough to fight with them and wrestle them back to the truth.

The struggle is painful, like a mother going through the pains of labor. Paul "gave birth" to the Galatian churches when their friendship was established. As they consider betrayal and he tries to win them back, it feels like labor all over again (4:19). Having been birthed into God's new creation, a law-based womb now beckons the Galatians back to the present evil age. They are listening to the tempting voice, and Paul is perplexed (4:19).

Paul tells the Galatians he will endure labor pains "until Christ is formed in you." The "you" is plural, which means Paul's focus is on Christ being formed in the Galatian churches. Martyn's translation reflects the plural "you," saying, "until Christ is formed in your congregations" (418). Paul desires Christ to be formed in the lives of individual Galatian believers as Christ has been formed in his own life (2:20), but individual formation always takes place within a larger communal formation. It will take more than individual Galatians to resist the Missionaries' message. A Christ-formed community is necessary to stay true to the gospel. When Christ is being formed in their churches, corporate resistance to the present evil age will gain momentum, and corporate witness to the new creation will become a way of life.

Though perplexed by their pending betrayal, Paul has not given up on the Galatians. He longs to be present with them (4:20) to embody a new creation witness and give rebirth to the Christ-formation process in their churches.

Life Lessons

The language of human slavery is understandable to people who battle addictions to drugs or alcohol. People oppressed through unjust political or economic systems resonate with Paul's talk of bondage. But for people who have not fallen into the enslaving trap of substance abuse and who have good jobs, nice houses, and comfortable lifestyles, Paul's assertion that all people are slaves sounds like an exaggeration.

Yet often our comfort proves to be the enslaving influence in our lives. Maintaining "our way of life" becomes more important than the way of Christ, which values sacrificial service above comfort. The "elemental spirits" twist self-interest into a cultural virtue, creating an economy where everyone literally must purchase more than they need if our economy is to survive. Enslaved to the things we own, we need liberation in order to keep our possessions in perspective and live lives of generosity.

The Spirit empowers us to resist cultural influences that are inconsistent with the gospel not by making us immune to these influences but by keeping us focused on God's work instead of our own. It is good for us to cry, "Abba! Father!" It is even better for us to listen to the Spirit make the same cry from within our hearts. The more we hear the Spirit's cry, the more our lives are shaped by God's love for us instead of the opinions of others. The more we listen to the Spirit, the less we listen to the present evil age.

Listening to the Spirit from within our hearts is a corporate activity. We need friends to help us hear what the Spirit is saying to us as individuals, and we need all our sisters and brothers to discern what the Spirit is saying to our congregations. Christ is formed within congregations and individual believers when friends listen together for the Spirit's voice in their midst.

1. Identify some of the things that enslave human beings.

_____
_____
_____
_____
_____
_____

2. How might the "elemental spirits" twist the "elemental principles" of Christian faith, causing us to focus on ourselves instead of God?

_____
_____
_____
_____
_____
_____

3. What practices or spiritual disciplines might help us listen to the Spirit cry, "Abba!" from within our hearts?

_____
_____
_____
_____

Freed Slaves, Adopted Children, and Friends

4. How can congregations listen for the Spirit's voice?

_____

_____

_____

_____

_____

5. In what ways do we make our faith law-based, seeking security in what we can do instead of in the Spirit's presence?

_____

_____

_____

_____

_____

6. When a friend dismisses our concerns for his or her well-being, how do we "appeal to our friendship" to help that friend listen?

_____

_____

_____

_____

_____

7. Why is friendship so important if Christ is to be formed in us corporately and individually?

_____

_____

_____

_____

8. What are the characteristics of a church where Christ is being formed in the congregation?

_____

_____

_____

_____

The Only Thing That Matters

Jesus often said, "Those who have ears, let them hear." Obviously he did not refer to physical hearing, but to a heart and soul level hearing that resulted in understanding. If the words go in one ear and out the other, a person has not truly "heard" the message, "for to hear God's word is to internalize that word, to understand it, and to obey it" (Longenecker, 207).

"Tell me, you who desire to be subject to the law, will you not listen to the law?" (4:21) Embraced by Christ through Paul's preaching and embracing Christ's faith with their own faith, the Galatians received ears to hear what God was saying to them. They now want to trade in their new ears for the old ones that are deaf to the deeper tones of God's truth. "Don't give up your new ears!" Paul seems to be saying. "Listen with your heart and you'll discover that the law backs me up."

Having already appealed to Abraham's obedience, the Missionaries probably contrast Abraham's sons, Isaac with Ishmael, to further their argument in favor of circumcision. Once again Paul turns the tables on them, this time using allegory instead of chronology to make his point. When he says what follows is an allegory (4:24), Paul is simply "saying that the story has a hidden significance, which he will now explain" (Hays, 302). The competition between Sarah and Hagar, Isaac and Ishmael, prefigures the current competition between Paul's law-free gospel and the Missionaries' law-observant message.

The hidden significance begins at conception. Despairing the absence of a son even after God's promise and realizing that they were not getting any younger, Abraham and Sarah concocted a plan. Trusting in his own flesh (strength), Abraham momentarily turned his back on God and had a son by Sarah's slave, Hagar. When the Missionaries proclaim their message, Paul hears the story of Abraham and Hagar in the background. The Missionaries' law-based message focuses on the flesh literally (circumcision) and figuratively (one's own strength in keeping the law). While the faith of Jesus is important, elements of human control remain essential in the Missionaries' vision of righteousness.

After the birth of his son by a slave woman, Abraham came to his senses and returned to God. Relying on the promises and relinquishing their own desire to control, Abraham and Sarah conceived a son. Isaac "was born through the promise" (4:23) because his parents trusted that God's promises would be fulfilled. With Isaac's conception, Abraham and Sarah relied on God's faithfulness instead of their own ability to control human events.

Hagar and Sarah represent two rival covenants in Paul's reading of the story, one being followed by Paul and the other by the Missionaries. While thinking they follow the covenant of law-observance grounded in Abraham's obedience, the Missionaries actually belong to Hagar's covenant of enslavement to the law. Paul associates Hagar with Mount Sinai and the giving of the law. All who enter this covenant (including the Galatians who are about to embrace the Missionaries' message) enter into slavery.

When Paul links Hagar with the present Jerusalem (4:25), he means the church in Jerusalem. Martyn observes, "Insofar as the Jerusalem church is at present allowing itself to serve as sponsor—or at least as an acquiescing ally—for the Law-observant Gentile mission, it stands in the slavery column" (439). James, Peter, and John, the "pillars" of the church (2:9), may not fully embrace the circumcision faction, but by tolerating and even bowing to this faction (2:11-14) they lean toward Hagar's covenant. Out of this Jerusalem-based and pillar-tolerated faction come the Missionaries, "bearing children for slavery" (4:24) in Galatia through their law-based message.

Since she corresponds "to the Jerusalem above" (4:26), Sarah bears children under the freedom of the new creation. In the Jerusalem above, life is lived according to God's will. When by the Spirit human beings do the will of God on earth as it is done in heaven, we give witness to the new creation/Jerusalem above. As witnesses to the new creation that is already present and to the Jerusalem above that will one day be fully revealed, we look to Sarah as "our mother" in the covenant of faith.

Connecting Sarah to the Jerusalem above leads Paul to Isaiah 54, an exilic passage pointing to new life through God's grace. After the barrenness of exile, Isaiah foresees a day of rejoicing when the children of Israel will be numerous again. The woman in Isaiah's poem represents Jerusalem, and "the cause of the woman's barrenness was her having been without a husband, that is to say without God's sustaining presence" (Martyn, 442). Though the promise seemed abandoned during the days of exile and though the law could not bring the promises to completion, all was not lost. Isaiah foresaw the day when God's presence would return to Jerusalem. In Paul's allegoric reading, Sarah represents Jerusalem's full experience of redemption from exile through Christ (3:13), an experience that already exists in the Jerusalem above.

Sarah/Jerusalem, barren no more but blessed with numerous children (4:27), corresponds to Paul's mission to the Gentiles, through which many children are being born into God's one new family. Jew and Gentile alike become children of the promise through Jesus. Like Isaac, they are born through God's faithfulness and not human striving.

Drive Them Out!

Like Isaac, the current children of the promise (and now the Spirit) face persecution from the children born according to the flesh (4:29). Genesis 21 says nothing about Ishmael persecuting Isaac and even suggests a normal sibling relationship that involves playing together (21:9). However, as the rabbis interpreted this story over the years, "playing" came to have a negative connotation, and it was assumed that Ishmael meant Isaac harm. Paul follows this tradition in saying that Ishmael persecuted Isaac.

Hagar's ancestors persecute Sarah's ancestors by calling them back to a life focused on law-keeping instead of promise-trusting. The Missionaries may sound sweet and sincere as they court the Galatians, but their flattering words are persecuting words in disguise.

In his most direct use of allegory, Paul applies a specific quotation from Sarah to the current situation. When Sarah demanded that Abraham evict Hagar and her son from the household, her words prefigured the church's response to those who insist on a law-based gospel. "But what does the scripture say? 'Drive out the slave and her child; for the child of the slave will not share the inheritance with the child of the free woman'" (4:30). Scripture takes Paul's side and *demands* that the Missionaries be driven from Galatia.

The issue of a law-based and a faith-based gospel is not an area where Paul can agree to disagree with his opponents, because the law-based gospel is really no gospel at all (1:7). To tolerate the Missionaries' position is to make the cross meaningless, "for if justification comes through the law, then Christ died for nothing" (2:21). The Missionaries exclude and keep out those whom Christ has included, promoting two families instead of one and requiring separate dinner tables for both families. For the sake of the gospel and the one family created through Christ, the excluders must be excluded.

In reality the Missionaries have already excluded themselves. By insisting on law observance for entrance into God's people, the Missionaries and those who follow them remove themselves from God's people. They shut themselves off from the Holy Spirit, since the Spirit comes through faith and not through the works of the law (3:2). The Spirit's presence identifies people as individuals of the promise who participate fully in the inheritance of Abraham (3:14, 29). The Spirit's absence indicates that the children "of the slave will not share the inheritance with the child of the free woman" (4:30). Paul's command to drive out the Missionaries simply acknowledges what the Missionaries have brought upon themselves.

Paul intentionally refers to Sarah as the "free woman" and Hagar as the "slave woman" in his allegorical treatment of their story. As advocates of Hagar's covenant, the Missionaries want to enslave the Galatians to the law. As members of Sarah's covenant, Paul urges the Galatians to resist the enslaving impulse, saying, "For freedom Christ has set us free. Stand firm, therefore, and do not submit again to a yoke of slavery" (5:1). Christ set us free from the present evil age, but the present evil age still exerts its influence. Those who have experienced freedom in the new creation must stand firm and resist the efforts of those who would have them submit to slavery again. The call to stand firm is a call to guard their freedom from the still encroaching present evil age.

Falling Away

Circumcision symbolizes the Missionaries' message and mobilizes Paul's resistance. Paul finally tackles the subject specifically in 5:2-4. If the Galatians embrace circumcision, then Christ will be of no benefit to them. The Missionaries do not deny the importance of

Christ's faith and the necessity of the human response of faith. What they deny is the sufficiency of faith. Law observance is also required for a Gentile to truly enter God's people. But to say that the faith of Jesus is lacking in any way to bring Jew and Gentile into right relationship with God and with each other is to deny the gospel altogether, in Paul's eyes. Instead of adding to their faith to make it stronger, the Galatians will deny their faith if they are circumcised, and Christ will then be of no benefit to them (5:2).

What the Galatians fail to realize and what the Missionaries are probably not telling them is that circumcision is but one of many requirements to which they are about to obligate themselves. If they are circumcised they will be "obliged to obey the entire law" (5:3), not just Sabbath restrictions, dietary laws, and the calendar of feasts and festivals. "My burden is light"(Matt 11:30), Jesus says, but the law's burden is heavy laden with strict requirements in every area of life. Instead of a person in whom Christ's life is lived, the Galatian male who is circumcised will become a Spirit-less debtor to the law "whose bill is always due" (Martyn, 470). Perpetual worry over whether a law has been transgressed will replace peaceful trust in the one who bore our transgressions. Through their embrace of the law, the Galatians will depart the new creation and enter a sphere of life that remains enslaved to the present evil age.

By cutting their foreskins the Galatians will actually cut themselves off from Christ (5:4). Circumcision as a parental option for reasons of hygiene or even religious significance is not a problem. Circumcision as a requirement for entrance into God's people is the issue. As practiced by the Missionaries, circumcision has salvific meaning and literally propels a man into the people of God. But to attach salvific significance to anything other than the faithfulness of Christ is to say that Christ's faith is insufficient. Instead of adding to God's grace by their own works, the Galatians will actually fall away from grace if they trust in anything other than Christ alone.

The Hope of Righteousness

Paul knows that true righteousness lies outside the realm of human accomplishment and belongs solely in the realm of divine gift. Righteousness is received, not achieved. The moment we trust our lives to the faith of Jesus, we receive right relationships with God and each other. However, because we remain sinners under the influence of the present evil age, we will not fully experience our righteousness until Christ returns. Thus our full experience of righteousness remains something we hope to receive in the future (5:5).

Daisaku Ikeda's children's story, *The Cherry Tree*, is set in postwar Japan. Two children come across an elderly man nursing a war-damaged cherry tree. When the children ask why he is tending an almost dead tree, he replies, "It's true she hasn't blossomed since before the war. But one day, with a little kindness and patience, she may again. Not in my lifetime perhaps, but one day! I'm sure of it" (as cited in Kenneson, 243).

Biblical hope is not an uncertain wish that something might come true. Our "hope of righteousness" exists because we trust God's faithfulness and, like Abraham, believe God's promises will be fulfilled. Such hope transforms us so that our present lives make little sense according to the present evil age but perfect sense in light of the new creation.

God does not require us to hope and trust on our own. The Spirit empowers and sustains our faith. Through the Spirit our faith is strengthened to wait for our full experience of Christ's righteousness (5:5). As we struggle to give witness to the new creation from within the present evil age, the Spirit "whispers" (Martyn, 472) encouragement into our hearts. The Missionaries say, "Rely on yourself and you will become righteous." The Spirit whispers, "Rely on God. God will sustain you until your hope of righteousness becomes reality."

The Only Thing That Matters

Ultimately circumcision does not matter, Paul says in 5:6, which is another way of saying what matters is the faith of Jesus. While we hope for righteousness, the Spirit empowers us to express and embody the faith of Jesus as our faith works through love. The greatest work is not circumcision or any other practice of Judaism. Love is the work to which God calls us, a love based not on our works but on the faith of Christ.

The love to which Paul refers is not an emotion or feeling, but a willingness to sacrifice for the good of one's sisters, brothers, and neighbors. It is Christ's faith that we work out through love, and Christ's ultimate display of faith and love took place on the cross. The Spirit produces sacrificial love within individuals and churches and thus works out the faith of Christ in the midst of the present evil age. Through such love the world sees glimpses of the new creation. The church then functions as a sign of the Jerusalem above and gives evidence of the hope of righteousness to come.

Knocked Off Track

In a foot race, competitors often seek an advantage by stepping in front of their opponents and cutting them off, either forcing them to slow down or causing them to stumble. The Galatians were running the good race of discipleship ("You were running well," 5:7) until the Missionaries cut them off and caused them to stumble. What makes no sense to Paul is that when the Galatians get up and dust themselves off, they follow the very people who knocked them down. They change course and are about to start a different race. By their "cut off" maneuver, the Missionaries prevent the Galatians from obeying the truth as Paul preaches it.

The "knock-down," course-diverting maneuver did not originate in the will of God (5:8). A small group of outsiders who do not have the Galatians' best interests in view exercise an influence far larger than their numbers (5:9). Most likely Paul has God's judgment in mind when he says the Missionaries "will pay the penalty" (5:10).

Paul does not give up on the Galatians. They may yet push aside the people who have knocked them down and return to the good race of faith. After explaining that the Missionaries have not come from God, he says, "I am confident about you in the Lord that you will not think otherwise" (5:10). Paul's confidence lies not in the Galatians' ability to come to their senses but in God's ability to wake them up. His confidence in them is "in the Lord," and through his letter Paul believes God will soften Galatian hearts.

The Missionaries apparently charge that Paul preaches circumcision. Most likely they refer to the episode Luke records in Acts 16:3, where Paul has Timothy circumcised to strengthen Timothy's ministry within the Jewish communities they visit. The charge is ludicrous. The persecution Paul receives on his missionary journeys (as recorded in Acts) most often comes at the hands of Jewish leaders threatened by Paul's law-free gospel. The Missionaries persecute Paul from afar by turning the Galatians from his friends into his enemies. Such persecution would be nonexistent if Paul preached circumcision. The offense of the cross creates the persecution, and the continuing presence of persecution sufficiently rebuts the charge that Paul preaches circumcision.

After remembering yet another false charge made against him, Paul vents his frustrations in a rather crude but highly symbolic manner. The Missionaries have sharpened their knives for the purpose of circumcising the Galatians. Paul suggests they would use their knives on themselves instead, saying, "I wish those who unsettle you would castrate themselves!" (5:12). The literal impotency thus rendered would symbolize the spiritual impotency of their message.

Life Lessons

Paul's use of allegory endorses a practice of Scripture reading familiar to many Christians. When reading a biblical story, passage, or verse, we often sense God speaking directly to our personal or church situation through what we read. The original intent of the writing has nothing to do with our current situation. Yet in God's hands the words of Scripture are living and active. The Spirit probes the depths of a biblical text to bring the specific word of guidance, correction, or encouragement that we need at the moment.

Our interpretations do not become part of God's word, as Paul's did. Thus we engage this practice with humility, recognizing our tendency to hear what we want to hear in the Bible. We guard against this tendency by bringing our interpretations before our sisters and brothers who help us discern what the Spirit is saying.

Often the word we need is one of hope. We live in a world of suffering, violence, and death. Love for God and love for neighbor do not characterize the times in which we live. When natural disaster strikes, our "hope of righteousness" reminds us that one day, creation will be at peace. When our sin and the sin of the world disrupts our relationships, the "hope of righteousness" tells us that one day, we will truly live in right relationship with God and with each other. When death interrupts our families, churches, and lives, our "hope of righteousness" reminds us that death has been defeated, and that one day we will fully experience Christ's victory.

1. While reading Scripture, have you ever heard a specific word from God that applied directly to a situation you were facing?

_____
_____
_____
_____
_____
_____

2. What are some obstacles that prevent us from hearing God's voice as we read Scripture?

_____
_____
_____
_____
_____
_____

3. Can you imagine a situation in which a congregation would have to "drive out" certain people from its fellowship?

_____
_____
_____
_____
_____
_____

4. Has there ever been a time when the "hope of righteousness" sustained you in the midst of great difficulty?

_____
_____
_____
_____
_____

5. In what ways can the "hope of righteousness" be twisted to encourage disengagement from the world and its suffering?

_____

_____

_____

_____

_____

_____

6. How can friends be vessels through which we hear the Spirit's whisper?

_____

_____

_____

_____

_____

_____

7. List concrete examples of "faith working through love."

_____

_____

_____

_____

_____

_____

8. What can cause a church to become impotent in its mission of giving witness to the new creation?

_____

_____

_____

_____

_____

_____

The Spirit Versus the Flesh

Galatians 5:13-26

Impotent for the purpose of producing righteousness, circumcision remains potent for the task of enslaving people to the law. The Galatians must remember their call to freedom if they are to stand firm against those who would submit them to slavery once more. The "you" of 5:13 is plural, which means Paul addresses churches and calls them to stand firm together. His use of "call" language points yet again to God's initiative. The call itself generates a new reality, transferring the Galatians into the realm of freedom established by Christ. Freedom is not something the Galatians have wrestled away from all the things that enslave them, but a call that places them squarely in God's new creation. Should they reject this call, they leave the new creation and cast their lot with the present evil age.

God's call to freedom does not create a zone where all personal choices are valid as long as they do not infringe upon anyone else's ability to make free personal choices. In setting us free from the present evil age, Jesus does not say, "You are now perfectly autonomous individuals, free to construct lives for yourselves however you see fit. Go ahead, decide what you want out of life and go for it!" Though the modern myth of the autonomous self says otherwise, Paul asserts that Jesus sets us free so that we can "through love become slaves to one another" (5:13). Freedom properly received leads to sacrifice for the neighbor, not indulgence of the self.

That the Galatians' personal experience of life will be diminished if they return to slavery is not the issue for Paul. Enslaved to a law that pours their energy into rule-keeping, the Galatians will be unable to truly love God and their neighbor. Human beings need deliverance from anything that privileges human over divine effort.

Until God's initiating love receives our full attention, we cannot truly love God with all our heart, soul, mind, and strength, and our neighbors as ourselves (5:14).

Obedience to the command that sums up the law is possible only as we trust the One who has completely fulfilled it. Through his life of complete communion with God and faithful fellowship with his neighbors, and through his sacrificial death on the cross, Jesus obeyed and fulfilled the whole law. As we trust the faithfulness of Jesus, we participate in his law-fulfilling life. As we live by the Spirit (5:16), Jesus lives his life of love for neighbor through us (2:20).

One indication that the Galatians had rejected the love of neighbor command, and thus their call to freedom, was their tendency to "bite and devour one another" (5:15). The phrase sounds strange until we think of any modern church that fights better than it loves. Of such churches we say, "They fight each other like cats and dogs." As in our day, in the ancient world it was common to use animal imagery in describing human patterns of behavior. When churches become consumed by fighting one another, they enslave themselves to their own "side" or "vision" instead of becoming slaves to each other through love.

The "Flesh"

To make matters much more difficult for the church, Paul says we contend with a force that encourages animal-like behavior and discourages sacrificial neighbor love. Where such behavior abounds, the "flesh" is at work. At various points in Galatians, Paul uses the word "flesh" to describe different things. Flesh can mean our bodies; Paul refers to the life he now lives in the flesh (2:20). Flesh can also mean the sinful inclination to focus on ourselves, so where the KJV speaks of creating "an occasion for the flesh" in 5:13, the NRSV says, "do not use your freedom as an opportunity for self-indulgence." The NIV translates the same verse as "do not use your freedom to indulge the sinful nature," using the definition of "flesh" as an actual sinful presence within us.

J. Louis Martyn argues that Paul personifies "flesh" in Galatians 5 and 6, viewing the flesh as a hostile spiritual power at work against God's purposes in the world. Instead of the sinful nature or sinful inclinations within individuals, Paul identifies a hostile power on the loose in Galatia. As with the elemental spirits of 4:3, the "flesh" personified is a way of naming the power of evil in the world. Evil is more than a product of sinful humanity. Literal evil forces in the spiritual realm work against God's intentions for creation and make ours a "present evil age."

Martyn's definition fits the overall context of Galatians. To use "flesh" as the "sinful nature" or "sinful inclinations" within a believer requires a shift from Paul's larger focus on communities. Personifying the "flesh" as a hostile spiritual power also connects with the notion of deliverance from "the present evil age," with its enslaving "elemental spirits."

Martyn translates 5:13 as "Do not allow freedom to be turned into a military base of operations for the Flesh, active as a cosmic power" (479). If the Galatians confuse freedom in Christ with freedom to live as they desire, they will create an open door through which the flesh will lead them away from God. Freedom conceived apart from slavery to one's sisters and brothers invites enslavement to the present evil age through the power of the flesh.

Live by the Spirit

The advance of the flesh in Galatia is part of its larger war against the Spirit. The flesh desires human enslavement to the present evil age. The Spirit desires human freedom in the new creation. These two forces oppose each other wherever they meet (5:16), and as Paul writes they are clashing in Galatia.

Again we note the difference a "flesh as hostile power" interpretation makes on how we understand Paul's meaning. Though individual believers certainly struggle against internal sinful inclinations, the flesh/Spirit battle in 5:16-17 "does not reflect some *internal struggle in the believer*" (Fee, 820). The forces of the present evil age assault the advance of God's new creation, and churches are at the forefront of the battlefield. Skirmishes are won when either side gains a greater shaping influence in the life of particular communities.

The Spirit is the more powerful force. Jesus defeated the flesh on the cross, and the current battle has no bearing on the war's final outcome. The Spirit struggles against the flesh to reveal God's new creation in the midst of the present evil age, and churches are the key point of visibility. For this reason the Spirit opposes the flesh "to prevent you from doing what you want" (5:17). The flesh turns communities into groups of individuals who do what they want, look out for number one, and ignore the call to love our neighbor. The Spirit opposes this focus-on-the-self influence, calling us instead to freedom lived out through neighbor-focused love and leading churches to live as signs of the new creation.

"Doing what you want" is a phrase the Galatians have probably heard before, because that is exactly what the Missionaries fear anyone will do without the law to restrain them. How can a people live morally upstanding lives without the guidance of the law? How can former pagans walk in the ways of God without God's law to show them the way? Such likely questions from the Missionaries make the law seem desirable, even necessary for Galatian churches fresh from old lives of paganism.

"Live by the Spirit" (5:16) is Paul's answer to the Missionaries' questions and also the means by which the Galatians resist the flesh, love one another, and give witness to the new creation. When individuals and communities allow the Spirit to lead them, no law is necessary to restrain or guide their behavior (5:18). A checklist of rules is irrelevant for a people from whom the Spirit cries, "Abba! Father!" and to whom the Spirit gives ability to love as God loves.

Joe English is the former drummer for the band Paul McCartney and Wings. English writes and performs music in the contemporary Christian genre. He always ends his concerts with a crowd-pleasing drum solo.

After English concluded a concert and was talking backstage with friends, a young boy made his way to English's drum set, picked up the sticks, and started hitting everything in sight. English rushed back to the stage but did not yell at the boy or jerk the sticks out of his hand. He sat down at the drum set, placed the boy in his lap, put the boy's hands in his own with the drum sticks still attached, and began to play. His hands guided by the great drummer, the boy played beautiful music. English gave an encore of his solo finale, only this time through the hands of a little boy (Roley, 70).

As individuals and churches, our part is not to play beautiful music on our own but to allow the Spirit to play beautiful music through us. Nor can we in our own strength prevent sour notes from sounding in our lives. Only to the extent that we live by the Spirit will we avoid gratifying the desires of the flesh (5:16). We resist the flesh by allowing the Spirit to fight through us. The initiative lies with God, who guides our lives by the Spirit.

The Works of the Flesh

Since the flesh as a hostile spiritual power is not visible to the human eye, its presence is known through the "works" it produces. When the flesh has a base of operations in a particular community, the works listed in 5:19-21 will be in evidence. The flesh has succeeded in distracting people from love of God and neighbor when these works appear.

Fornication refers to marital unfaithfulness of a sexual nature, as does the reference to impurity. Licentiousness builds on the first two works to produce "uncontrolled debauchery . . . prideful flaunting" (Martyn, 496) of sexual immorality. The flesh twists God's wonderful gift of sexual intimacy between husband and wife into an individual demand for sexual fulfillment. To participate in fornication, impurity, and licentiousness is to treat people of the opposite sex as objects for one's own personal gratification instead of neighbors to whom one is enslaved through love. Where the flesh produces such works, love of neighbor is greatly diminished.

Idolatry and sorcery (5:20) appear whenever people place their trust in something or someone other than God. Whether through idols representing pagan gods in Paul's day or the idols of money, sex, and power in our own, the flesh is ever creative in shifting human trust onto untrustworthy human objects. The sorcerer's spell may come from black magic or illegal narcotics, but for those so entranced the result is the same: a flesh-dominated life of addiction from which only the Spirit can bring release.

The middle eight works on the list of fifteen directly rip communities apart. When "enmities, strife, jealousy, anger, quarrels, dissensions, factions, envy" are present, the hold of the flesh is strong and the ability to love is weak. If people are jealous or envious of their sisters and brothers, becoming slaves to one another through love will not be a high priority.

Through drunkenness and carousing people exchange the influence of the Spirit for the influence of alcohol, blocking the Spirit's advance into the present evil age and hiding the new creation in a drunken stupor. Paul ends the list with the phrase "and things like these," indicating the list is representative and not exhaustive. Anything the flesh uses to weaken communities is a work of the flesh. When given the opportunity, the flesh can use anything to decrease love for God and neighbor.

"I am warning you, as I warned you before: those who do such things will not inherit the kingdom of God" (5:21). After receiving God's gifts, a community cannot spit in the face of the gift-giver without incurring judgment (Martyn, 498). Those who continually embrace the works of the flesh, showing no remorse or desire for repentance, have no share in the kingdom inheritance made available through Jesus' faithfulness.

John Calvin asks, "But this makes it sound as if all are cut off from hope of salvation; for who is there who does not labour under one or other of these sins?" (104) Indeed, which is why right relationship with God comes through Jesus' faithfulness, not our own. Works of the flesh still occasionally flow from communities and individuals that live by the Spirit, but once recognized, confession and repentance follow. However, the ability to recognize the works of the flesh and resist the flesh's influence declines the more a person or people depend on themselves instead of God. As the Galatians contemplate exchanging dependence on the Spirit for independent obedience to the law, Paul warns them of the dangers that lie ahead.

The Fruit of the Spirit

The works of the flesh tear down communities; by contrast, the fruit of the Spirit build up communities and strengthen their new creation witness. Where love for neighbor abounds, a community reflects God's love. Where joy flows from the Spirit instead of circumstances, a community's focus on God remains strong. When peace, understood not as the absence of conflict but the presence of trust in God and each other, reigns in a church, the flesh has little room to maneuver. Congregational patience strengthens the hope of the righteousness to come and produces grace when people fail to live in right relationship with God and with each other. When kindness, generosity, faithfulness, gentleness, and self-control characterize a church, its members embrace each other and their neighbors with a love that can only come from God.

A community cannot reflect the fruit of the Spirit if the fruit have not grown within its individual members. But neither can the individual receive the Spirit's fruit apart from the community, since the fruit are relational in nature. While receiving the Spirit's fruit contributes to the individual's experience of abundant life, "nurturing individual fruit in individual lives is not our ultimate goal. Instead, the church is called to embody before the world in all its relationships the kind of reconciled and transformed life that God desires for all creation" (Kenneson, 34). Within the context of community, individuals seek spiritual growth not primarily for their own benefit but for the health of the community, so that the Spirit's new creation witness will be strengthened in their church home.

The flesh produces works, but the Spirit produces fruit. As people allow themselves to be shaped by the flesh, they produce works from within themselves that reflect the present evil age. By contrast, the Spirit goes beyond influencing our works to producing the fruit we cannot produce ourselves. While love is certainly something we do, as a fruit of the Spirit it is something we receive in order to share. Kindness is a practice to which we are called, but it is also a fruit the Spirit develops in us. Generous giving is an act of the will, but as a fruit of the Spirit it becomes a part of who we are. Fruit grows as a community focuses less on its own work and more on the Spirit's work in its midst.

"There is no law against such things," Paul says of the Spirit's fruit when he finishes the list (5:23). The law restrains people from doing certain things but not the things Paul has just mentioned. Paul's point is that the law can restrain behavior but it cannot produce fruit. The Spirit does more than demand obedience; it makes obedience possible by empowering individuals and communities. There is no need "to say, 'don't covet,' to those who are actively pursuing the good of others out of kindness" (Fee, 453). The law may keep out an occasional weed, but it will never produce fruit like the Spirit.

The Work of the Farmer

When my grandfather was thirteen years old, his family moved off the farm and into the city. He loves to tell of how happy he was that day. He was old enough to know that farm work is hard work, and he gladly exchanged the work of the farm for the work of the mill. Many farmers love the work, of course, including my great-grandfather who spent the rest of his life trying to get back on the farm. But all agree that the farming life is a difficult life, demanding a family's full attention and greatest effort.

No matter how hard farmers work, though, they cannot make the sun shine, the clouds rain, or the seeds sprout. Though indispensable to the process, the farmer cannot produce the growth. In the same way, we cannot produce the Spirit's fruit in our communities, but our hard work is still required.

The Spirit cannot produce fruit until people crucify the flesh and its passions (5:24). We crucify the flesh through the hard work of not relying on our hard work but trusting in Jesus' work on our behalf. Paul refers to our initial trust in the faith of Jesus and the baptism that follows. Through faith and baptism we participate in Christ's cross, where he crucified and thus defeated the flesh. As we embrace Christ's faith and enter his baptism, God plants the seeds of the Spirit's fruit.

Through weekly corporate worship, the community celebrates Christ's victory and renews its baptismal commitments. The hard work of preparing our hearts, showing up whether we feel like it or not, and giving our best to God creates room for the Spirit's fruit to grow. Corporate worship provides "a kind of foothold for the Spirit's work, a foothold that can be nurtured and expanded to embrace the rest of our lives" (Kenneson, 33). As we sing, pray, and hear God's word read and proclaimed, the Spirit waters the seeds and causes the fruit to grow.

Just as seeds need sunlight, the seeds planted at baptism need the light of God's word for growth to occur. "If we live by the Spirit," Paul says, "let us also be guided by the Spirit" (5:25). The Spirit speaks to our hearts as we read, study, and listen to God's word. The Spirit speaks with a whisper as we listen to God in prayer. Fruit grows when a community sits still long enough to listen to the Spirit's voice and then follows wherever the Spirit leads.

Pulling weeds and pruning plants characterize life on the farm and life in the Spirit. As evidence of growth develops, a community can easily take its eyes off the Spirit and deceive itself into thinking the growth is self-generated. Such deception quickly leads to conceit, competition, and envy (5:26). Communities and individuals must work hard to pull the weeds of selfishness and self-absorption. They must work hard to prune the dead growth of apathy and complacency.

The farmer cannot produce the growth, but the farmer's work enhances the environment in which growth can occur. As we enter the seedbed of baptism, soak in the nourishing waters of worship and the Spirit-guided light of the word, and pull the weeds of conceit, competition, and envy, we enhance the congregational and personal environments in which the Spirit's fruit can grow.

The Missionaries call the Galatians to the hard work of law-keeping, where everything revolves around their ability to obey. Paul calls them to the hard work of farming, where life revolves around the Spirit's ability to produce growth and where their hard work is a grateful response to God's gracious initiative.

Life Lessons

Awareness of the presence of evil in the world and within each of us elbows its way into our daily consciousness. Sometimes we attempt to ignore evil. Sometimes we feel overwhelmed by its power. Sometimes we question how God can allow evil to exist. In the midst of our questions and varying emotional responses to evil, the more ways we can name and image the evil among us, the more the Spirit can combat evil through us.

Interpreting the flesh as a hostile power at work in the world helps us remember the reality of spiritual evil. We need not look for a literal "flesh" that has physical characteristics we see with our eyes. Instead, when we see "the works of the flesh" in our lives, our churches, and our world, we know that spiritual evil has combined with human sinfulness to resist the will of God.

We know the Spirit battles against the flesh, and we know the Spirit's ultimate victory is assured. Yet we struggle with our own efforts to participate in the battle, exactly because we give too much weight to our own efforts. Spiritual disciplines and practices (spiritual farm work) prepare the soil for the Spirit's fruit-growing work in us.

These disciplines (corporate worship, prayer, Bible study, fellowship, service, etc.) are thus a means to an end, not ends in themselves. When we practice spiritual disciplines to prove our discipline, the harvest of fruit from the Spirit will be minimal and our frustration great. When spiritual disciplines are engaged to increase our attentiveness to God instead of to get God's attention by our good works, the Spirit draws us into the life of God and produces fruit in abundance.

1. How do Christians and churches abuse or misuse God's call to freedom?

_____

_____

_____

_____

_____

2. If we are slaves to one another through love, then our use of time will be transformed. How much time do you devote each day to your own agenda, needs, and desires? How much time do you devote to the needs of others?

_____

_____

_____

_____

_____

3. How do churches and individuals unknowingly create within themselves a base of operations for the flesh?

_____

_____

_____

_____

_____

4. Perhaps you do not agree with the "flesh as hostile power" interpretation. If not, make the case for interpreting the flesh as our sinful nature/inclinations in 5:13-21.

_____

_____

_____

_____

_____

5. Why does the Spirit develop fruit in us as people-in-community instead of as isolated individuals?

_____

_____

_____

_____

_____

6. How would you respond to the individual who says that he or she does not need to attend church because worship can take place anywhere and at any time?

_____

_____

_____

_____

_____

7. Have you ever felt guilty for not being patient, kind, or exercising enough self-control? How can the fact that these fruit are gifts of the Spirit and not traits we develop on our own change the way you understand moments when such fruit are absent in your life?

_____

_____

_____

_____

_____

8. Who do you know that reflects an abundance of one or more of the Spirit's fruit? Describe how these fruit are visible in that person's life.

_____

_____

_____

_____

10

Fruit on Display

Galatians 6:1-18

Have you ever longed for the perfect church? Have you ever been frustrated or disappointed by the behavior of church members and the unhealthy functioning of churches? As Paul presents the wonderful list of the Spirit's fruit, and as we realize these fruit are gifts and not achievements, we wonder why we so rarely see such fruit in our communities. Could it be that the Spirit withholds fruit for some reason we cannot understand, or does the fault lie with our farming efforts? In reality, the source of our disappointment begins with our expectations. The fruit of the Spirit are not given to make us sinless, nor are they tools with which we construct our ideal fellowship. The Spirit grows fruit within sinful congregations that still struggle with the patterns, habits, and works of the flesh. The presence of fruit does not indicate that a church has left the present evil age. The fruit of the Spirit enable sinful congregations to point to God's new creation and to the Christ who makes all things new.

Fruit-filled communities know they still sin, and out of the Spirit's fruit they know how to faithfully restore sinners (6:1). Paul speaks to "you who have received the Spirit," meaning every member of the Galatian congregations. When a person "is detected in a transgression," the congregation relies on the fruit of gentleness (5:23) in leading that person through the process of confession, repentance, and full restoration into the fellowship. Where the fruit of gentleness abounds, "sinners" are not publicly condemned as negative examples nor are they privately convicted in parking lot gossip gatherings. The "sinner" is a cherished member of the family without whom the church's witness suffers. For the health of the individual and the church, the "sinner" is restored in a spirit of gentleness.

The Babemba tribe in South Africa has an unusual way of administering justice. A person who has acted irresponsibly or done something wrong is placed alone at the center of the village. All work ceases, and everyone gathers in a large circle around the accused. Then each person, one by one, speaks to the "sinner" about all the good things he or she has done in his or her lifetime. Every experience that can be recalled is shared with as much accuracy as possible. All positive attributes, generous deeds, strengths, and acts of kindness are recited carefully and at length. The ceremony often lasts several days and does not end until everyone is drained of all possible positive comments regarding the person in question. Then the circle is broken, a celebration is held, and the person is welcomed back into the tribe (McCullough, *Pelicans*, 98).

If the Galatians enter life under the law, then they will never experience anything remotely resembling a Babemba tribe restoration ceremony. The fruit of gentleness will be an exotic plant that never arrives at their tables. The competition, rigidity, and need to punish rule-breakers that accompanies life under the law will lead them to cast stones at the accused instead of compliments. But if they give the Spirit's fruit room to grow by relying on God instead of their law-keeping ability, gentleness with each other will blossom. They may even have good things to say when someone is "detected in a transgression."

"It Could Happen to You"

"Take care that you yourselves are not tempted," Paul warns at the end of 6:1, which is another way of saying that the "sinner" is no better or worse than anyone else in the family. When a person is detected in a transgression, Paul knows some people will think, "I could never do something like that." These are the same people who think they are better than others (4:3) and build themselves up through comparisons with their sisters and brothers (4:4). They have neglected the hard work of weeding and pruning. The fruit of gentleness has no room to grow, and they have no business participating in the restoration of a transgressor.

Believers in whom the Spirit's fruit grow abundantly test their own work instead of the work of others (6:4). When tests reveal the Spirit's fruit in their lives, believers give thanks to God. When tests reveal weeds that need pulling, believers rely on the Spirit and get to work. Believers test themselves not to mark their personal progress on a spiritual growth chart, but to make sure they are giving their best to God and to the congregation.

Believers should get used to testing their own works now, because at the final judgment comparing one's works to another person's will not be an option. "For all must carry their own loads," Paul says in 6:5, referring to the day when God will judge the works of all people. Righteousness will not be determined by one's works on the final day, but by one's reception of Jesus' work. The final testing of works communicates the seriousness of sin and the nonnegotiable call to service, without in any way suggesting that righteousness depends on passing the test. Paul speaks good news to the Galatians: they matter enough to God that God actually cares about how they live and expects them to do their part in the church's witness.

Bearing Burdens

The Galatians will carry their own loads at the final judgment, but for now they carry each other's burdens (6:2). Relying on the fruit developed by the Spirit in their communities, Spirit-led people find a way to strengthen, encourage, and uplift their sisters and brothers. If the Galatians offer such sacrificial service to each other, they will participate in Christ's law-fulfilling sacrificial life and death. Jesus bore the burden of human sinfulness on the cross, and the bearing of burdens within Christian communities reflects Christ's sacrifice.

Perhaps the Missionaries have successfully convinced the Galatians not to bear the financial burdens of their teachers in the faith. After departing the Galatian region, Paul most likely left behind teachers to lead and disciple the new congregations. When the Galatians began leaning toward the Missionaries and their anti-Paul message, the first group to suffer would logically be the teachers Paul left behind. To counter this consequence, Paul says, "Those who are taught the word must share in all good things with their teacher" (6:6).

Reaping What They Sow

The judgment theme continues in 6:7. Should the Galatians embrace the law, they will mock God, arguing that their own obedience must be added to Christ's faithfulness if they are to be righteous. By their actions they would say to God, "What Jesus has done according to your will is not enough." Such mocking will not go unnoticed, Paul warns. The Galatians will reap what they sow.

"If you sow to your own flesh, you will reap corruption from the flesh," Paul says in 6:8. Notice the emphasis on *your own* flesh. Paul switches definitions at this point, no longer referring to the flesh as a hostile power. Does he now speak of the flesh as the physical body or as the sinful nature/inclination within each person? If he uses the sinful nature definition, then sowing to the flesh would be entering a life of self-indulgence. Paul earlier warns against such a lifestyle (5:21), but here his interest is in the change of focus the Galatians are considering. "Your own flesh" refers to the physical body and to the physical act of circumcision the Galatians contemplate. If they sow to the flesh through circumcision, they will reap corruption by trusting law-observance instead of God.

When they trust in the faithfulness of Christ alone, the Galatians sow to the Spirit as they invite the Spirit to guide them and grow fruit in their communities. They will reap eternal life not through their own ability to live by the Spirit, but through their trust in Jesus. Hays suggests that the phrase "you will reap eternal life from the Spirit" (6:8) refers to the resurrection of the body (336). Eternal life is from the Spirit, since through the Spirit God will resurrect the dead in Christ on the last day. The bodily reference also connects with the bodily definition of flesh Paul uses in 6:8.

Combating Weariness

Are the Galatians open to the Missionaries' message because they have grown weary of doing good? Do the rigors of the law sound more appealing than the exhausting rigors of love? If so, we can understand. When we think of all the needs of a war-torn impoverished world within which the church gives witness to God's peaceful, plentiful new creation, paralysis can easily set in. When we think of the needs in our own families and church families, weariness comes upon us quickly.

Paul does not say, "So let us not grow weary in doing what is right, because if we keep trying we will eventually make a difference." He does not say, "I know it's hard, but be optimistic; your breakthrough is just around the corner." Paul says we guard against weariness when we remember "we will reap at harvest-time" (6:9). At harvest time, life will be as God intends it to be, and we will fully experience the new creation to which we have given witness through doing what is right.

As we wait for the harvest time, we strive to make a difference in a world of war and suffering and in our families of pain and longing. Paul does not endorse resigning ourselves to the way things are because we will reap at harvest time only "if we do not give up." Instead, he places the focus on God's initiative in the coming of the kingdom and emphasizes our role as witnesses to Christ and his new creation. Paul says nothing about the results of our works because the results are up to God. Our part is to do what is right and to work for the good of all (especially our sisters and brothers in the church) whenever we have the opportunity (6:10). Instead of a law to fulfill, God gives us the Spirit to receive and a world to love.

Summing It Up

I write these words on a computer, and with the click of a mouse I can *italicize*, underline, and **boldface** text. If I want to draw your attention to a certain phrase, I can easily make that phrase stand out from the rest of the page.

As he writes the Galatians, Paul obviously does not have a computer, but he does have a secretary. He dictates his letter and someone else writes it down. But as he arrives at the last section of the letter and his last chance to get across his point, Paul stops dictating and starts writing. "See what large letters I make when I am writing in my own hand!" (6:11) Paul wants his final appeal to stand out from the rest of the letter. The larger letters he forms with his own hand signal that what follows is more than a stale conclusion. The whole of Paul's argument is summed up in this conclusion with the expectation that God will act when these words are read to the Galatian congregations.

Paul begins his conclusion with one last testimony against the Missionaries. Their care for the Galatians is limited, but their care for themselves knows no bounds. They want converts to brag about, and the more men they circumcise the greater their "showing in the flesh" (6:12). The Missionaries have no interest in obeying every aspect of the law (6:13) and great interest in making a name for themselves.

Such self-focus insures that the Missionaries will never be acquainted with persecution for the cross's sake. By contrast, Paul confesses, "I carry the marks of Jesus branded on my body" (6:17). He refers not to an early Christian tattoo but to the beatings and whippings he has endured for the sake of the gospel. In previous missionary journeys, Paul often aroused opposition with his preaching and endured bodily harm from those threatened by his message. His body bears the evidence of this persecution even as he writes with his own hand. The contrast between Paul and the Missionaries poses a question for the Galatians. Do they want to be used by Missionaries who do not have their best interests at heart, or do they want to embrace the missionary who believes so strongly in his message that he faces bodily harm for the sake of the gospel?

The Cross and the New Creation

The Missionaries boast of converts, but Paul boasts of the cross (6:14). The cross is the central event of the gospel Paul proclaims and the central event that has transformed his life. Paul says that by the cross of Christ, "the world has been crucified to me, and I to the world" (6:14). He no longer cares about what the world thinks of him, which means he has no interest in bragging about his number of converts. He no longer follows the worldly temptation to base his life on his own accomplishments. Now he places his confidence and hope in the cross and in the faithfulness of the One who on the cross "gave himself for our sins" (1:4).

Worldly religious markers such as circumcision no longer have meaning for Paul and for all who trust Jesus' faithfulness. Now, the new creation established through Christ's cross and resurrection is everything (6:15)! On the surface, nothing has changed because the present evil age still exists. But people who live by the Spirit know that "a new reality has been brought into being that determines the destiny of the whole creation" (Hays, 344) because "the God who created the world has come to reclaim and transform it" (Martyn, 345).

The elemental spirits still corrupt human systems and enslave people. The flesh still battles against the Spirit and promotes a self-focus instead of a God and neighbor focus. The present evil age is alive and well. But its days are numbered. Its ultimate demise was accomplished on the cross. Even now the new creation advances into territory previously held by the present age, and one day God will unveil the new creation for all to see. All will be as God intends creation to be. Until then, as Christian communities live by the Spirit, love their neighbors, and work for the good of all, they say with Paul that new creation is everything!

Farewell

Paul knows his letter will not be received with universal rejoicing and applause. Some will continue their leanings toward the Missionaries and reject Paul in the process. He does not extend his departing word of peace to them, but only to "those who will follow this rule" (6:16), living lives that point to the new creation.

Not all will be persuaded, but some, perhaps most, will. Paul remains confident that the Galatians will not follow the Missionaries down the road of law. He extends the grace of Christ to his "brothers and sisters" in 6:18, which means they remain family. The Galatian communities have heard from a brother, and a brother's word will carry greater weight than the words of the Missionaries.

Paul's confidence is not in his own word or in the Galatians' willingness to hear his word. God's word has been proclaimed through Paul's words. Paul ends his letter with the word "amen," signaling the end of a sermon in which God has been present and active. As the Galatian congregations hear Paul's letter read during corporate worship, God is at work focusing their attention on the faithfulness of Jesus. God draws their focus away from human achievement, anchors them in the new creation, and fills them with the Holy Spirit. God continues to do the same today whenever communities listen to God's voice through Paul's Letter to the Galatians. May it be so for your church and mine. Amen.

Life Lessons

The idea of "detecting" a person's sins, confronting the person, and then restoring him or her sounds noble but creates uncomfortable feelings within us. Our cultural emphasis on personal privacy and "minding our own business" makes the process Paul describes in 6:1 a foreign procedure. Our first thoughts often drift toward the very real possibility that the process could be abused.

But the main reason we hesitate to name each other's sins flows from the intimate fellowship required. Naming each other's sins requires an involvement in each other's lives that goes beyond the surface level of relating with which we are accustomed in our churches. We prefer to keep our distance.

But when the fruit of the Spirit grows in abundance, the naming of sins reflects the depth of a church's fellowship. Sin harms the well-being of the individual and weakens the church's corporate witness. Because each person is a treasured member of the community and because the community's corporate witness is so valuable, naming sins and restoring the sinner is a crucial practice if churches want to give witness to the new creation.

Since the new creation is everything, anything that weakens a church's experience of and witness to the new creation must be addressed. Through the Spirit, the community restores the fallen and encourages the weary. Through the Spirit, the community boasts only in the cross and not in their own work. Through the Spirit, the community trusts in the faithfulness of Jesus.

1. Naming each other's sins is not something a church assigns to a committee. Because the practice is so foreign to our Christian experience, it is probably best to first experiment on an individual level. Is there someone you trust enough to name your sins, and who trusts you to name theirs?

_____

_____

_____

_____

_____

_____

_____

2. When someone has been publicly detected in a transgression, have you ever thought, "I could never do something like that." How can you avoid such thoughts?

_____

_____

_____

_____

_____

_____

_____

3. Taking a cue from the Babemba tribe, what are some creative ways in which churches can restore people who have publicly fallen?

_____
_____
_____
_____
_____
_____

4. How can friends help each other test their own works?

_____
_____
_____
_____
_____
_____

5. The needs never end, and the workers always seem too few. How can churches help their ministers and lay workers avoid growing weary in doing what is right?

_____
_____
_____
_____
_____
_____

6.What are the needs of the world that make you feel tired when you think about them, and how can you avoid paralysis in the face of these needs?

_____
_____
_____
_____
_____

Fruit on Display

7. In what ways do churches and individuals try to "make a good showing" to impress their peers?

_____

_____

_____

_____

_____

_____

8. How can we help ourselves boast of the cross and not our own "accomplishments?"

_____

_____

_____

_____

_____

_____

Bibliography

Baker, Mark D. *Religious No More*. Downers Grove IL: InterVarsity, 1999.

Berry, Wendell. *Jayber Crow*. Washington, DC: Counterpoint, 2000.

Betz, Hans Deiter. *Galatians: A Commentary on Paul's Letter to the Churches in Galatia*. Hermeneia. Philadelphia: Fortress, 1979.

Bruce, F. F. *The Epistle to the Galatians: A Commentary on the Greek Text*. NIGTC. Grand Rapids: Eerdmans, 1982.

Calvin, John. *The Epistles of Paul the Apostle to the Galatians, Ephesians, Philippians, and Colossians*. T. H. L. Parker, translator. London: Oliver and Boyd, 1965.

Charry, Ellen. *By the Renewing of Your Minds*. New York: Oxford University Press, 1999.

Cousar, Charles B. *Galatians*. Interpretation. Atlanta: John Knox, 1982.

Dawn, Marva. *Powers, Weakness, and the Tabernacling of God*. Grand Rapids: Eerdmans, 2001.

———— and Eugene Peterson. *The Unnecessary Pastor*. Grand Rapids: Eerdmans, 2000.

Fee, Gordon. *God's Empowering Presence*. Peabody MA: Hendrickson, 1994.

Harink, Douglas. *Paul Among the Postliberals: Pauline Theology Beyond Christendom and Modernity*. Grand Rapids: Brazos, 2003.

Hays, Richard B. "The Letter to the Galatians." In vol. 11 of *The New Interpreter's Bible*, 181-348. Nashville: Abingdon, 2000.

Kenneson, Philip D. *Life on the Vine: Cultivating the Fruit of the Spirit in Christian Community.* Downers Grove IL: InterVarsity, 1999.

Longenecker, Richard N. *Galatians.* WBC 41. Dallas: Word, 1990.

Martyn, J. Louis. *Galatians.* AB 33A. New York: Doubleday, 1997.

McCullough, Donald. *The Trivialization of God.* Colorado Springs: NavPress, 1995.

―――. *The Wisdom of Pelicans.* New York: Penguin, 2002.

Morris, Edmund. *Theodore Rex.* New York: Random House, 2001.

Peterson, Eugene. "Keynote Address." Montreat Preachers Conference. Montreat NC, May 29–June 2, 2000.

Roley, Scott. *God's Neighborhood.* Downers Grove IL: InterVarsity, 2004.

Tyson, Timothy B. *Blood Done Sign My Name.* New York: Crown, 2004.

Wright, N. T. *The Climax of the Covenant: Christ and the Law in Pauline Theology.* Minneapolis: Fortress, 1993.